STATUTORY INTERPRETATION: GENERAL PRINCIPLES AND RECENT TRENDS

LAWS AND LEGISLATION SERIES

LAWS AND LEGISLATION SERIES

STATUTORY INTERPRETATION: GENERAL PRINCIPLES AND RECENT TRENDS

YULE KIM

Nova Science Publishers, Inc.
New York

LIBRARY OF CONGRESS CATALOGING-IN-PUBLICATION DATA

Available Upon Request

ISBN: 978-1-60692-997-1

Published by Nova Science Publishers, Inc. ✝ New York

CONTENTS

PREFACE*

The Supreme Court has expressed an interest "that Congress be able to legislate against a background of clear interpretive rules, so that it may know the effect of the language it adopts." This report identifies and describes some of the more important rules and conventions of interpretation that the Court applies. Although this report focuses primarily on the Court's methodology in construing statutory text, the Court's approach to reliance on legislative history are also briefly described.

In analyzing a statute's text, the Court is guided by the basic principle that a statute should be read as a harmonious whole, with its separate parts being interpreted within their broader statutory context in a manner that furthers statutory purpose. The various canons of interpretation and presumptions as to substantive results are usually subordinated to interpretations that further a clearly expressed congressional purpose.

The Court frequently relies on "canons" of construction to draw inferences about the meaning of statutory language. For example, in considering the meaning of particular words and phrases, the Court distinguishes between terms of art that may have specialized meanings and other words that are ordinarily given a dictionary definition. Other canons direct that all words of a statute be given effect if possible, that a term used more than once in a statute should ordinarily be given the same meaning throughout, and that specific statutory language ordinarily trumps conflicting general language. "Ordinarily" is a necessary caveat, since any of these "canons" gives way if context reveals an evident contrary meaning.

Not infrequently the Court stacks the deck, and subordinates the general, linguistic canons of statutory construction, as well as other interpretive principles, to overriding presumptions that favor particular substantive results. The Court

---

* This is an edited, excerpted and augmented edition of a Congressional Research Service publication Order Code 97-589, dated August 31, 2008.

usually requires a "clear statement" of congressional intent to negate one of these presumptions. A commonly invoked presumption is that Congress does not intend to change judge-made law. Other presumptions disfavor preemption of state law and abrogation of state immunity from suit in federal court. Congress must also be very clear if retroactive application of a statute or repeal of an existing law is intended. The Court tries to avoid an interpretation that would raise serious doubts about a statute's constitutionality. Other presumptions that are overridden only by "clear statement" of congressional intent are also identified and described.

This report sets forth a brief overview of the Supreme Court's approach to statutory interpretation.[1] The bulk of the report describes some of the Court's more important methods of construing statutory text, and the remainder briefly describes the Court's restraint in relying on legislative history. The Court has expressed an interest "that Congress be able to legislate against a background of clear interpretive rules, so that it may know the effect of the language it adopts."[2] In reading statutes, the Supreme Court applies various rules and conventions of interpretation, and also sometimes superimposes various presumptions favoring particular substantive results. Other conventions assist the Court in determining whether or not to consider legislative history. Although there is some overlap and inconsistency among these rules and conventions, and although the Court's pathway through the mix is often not clearly foreseeable, an understanding of interpretational possibilities may nonetheless lessen the burdens of statutory drafting and aid Congress in choosing among various drafting options.

Executive Order 12988, which provides guidance to executive agencies on preparing legislation, contains a useful checklist of considerations to keep in mind when drafting legislation.[3] Many items on the checklist are topics addressed in this report, and many of the court decisions cited under those topics have resulted from the absence of clear statutory guidance. Consideration of the checklist may facilitate clarification of congressional intent and may thereby lessen the need for litigation as a means to resolve ambiguity in legislation.

Of course, Congress can always amend a statute to require a result different from that reached by the Court. In interpreting statutes, the Court recognizes that legislative power resides in Congress, and that Congress can legislate away interpretations with which it disagrees.[4] Congress has revisited statutory issues fairly frequently in order to override or counter the Court's interpretations.[5] Corrective amendment can be a lengthy and time-consuming process, however, and Congress in most instances will probably wish to state its intent clearly the first time around.

Chapter 1

STATUTORY TEXT

IN GENERAL — STATUTORY CONTEXT AND PURPOSE

The starting point in statutory construction is the language of the statute itself. The Supreme Court often recites the "plain meaning rule," that, if the language of the statute is clear, there is no need to look outside the statute to its legislative history in order to ascertain the statute's meaning.[6] It was once axiomatic that this "rule" was honored more in the breach than in the observance. However, the Court has begun to place more emphasis on statutory text and less emphasis on legislative history and other sources "extrinsic" to that text. More often than before, statutory text is the ending point as well as the starting point for interpretation.

A cardinal rule of construction is that a statute should be read as a harmonious whole, with its various parts being interpreted within their broader statutory context in a manner that furthers statutory purposes. Justice Scalia, who has been in the vanguard of efforts to redirect statutory construction toward statutory text and away from legislative history, has aptly characterized this general approach. "Statutory construction . . . is a holistic endeavor. A provision that may seem ambiguous in isolation is often clarified by the remainder of the statutory scheme — because the same terminology is used elsewhere in a context that makes its meaning clear, or because only one of the permissible meanings produces a substantive effect that is compatible with the rest of the law."[7] This was not a novel approach. In 1850 Chief Justice Taney described the same process: "In expounding a statute, we must not be guided by a single sentence or member of a sentence, but look to the provisions of the whole law, and to its object and policy."[8] Thus, the meaning of a specific statutory directive may be shaped, for example, by that statute's definitions of terms, by the statute's statement of findings and purposes, by the directive's relationship to other specific directives, by purposes inferred from those directives or from the statute as a whole, and by the statute's overall structure. Courts also look to the broader context of the body of law into which the enactment fits.[9]

The Supreme Court occasionally relies on general rules or canons of construction in resolving statutory meaning. The Court, moreover, presumes "that Congress legislates with knowledge of our basic rules of statutory construction."[10] This report sets forth a number of such rules, conventions, and presumptions that the Court has relied on. It is well to keep in mind, however, that the overriding objective of statutory construction is to effectuate statutory purpose. As Justice Jackson put it more than 50 years ago, "[h]owever well these rules may serve at times to decipher legislative intent, they long have been subordinated to the doctrine that courts will construe the details of an act in conformity with its dominating general purpose, will read text in the light of context and will interpret the text so far as the meaning of the words fairly permits so as to carry out in particular cases the generally expressed legislative policy."[11]

Chapter 2

CANONS OF CONSTRUCTION

IN GENERAL

"[C]anons of construction are no more than rules of thumb that help courts determine the meaning of legislation, and in interpreting a statute a court should always turn first to one, cardinal canon before all others. . . . [C]ourts must presume that a legislature says in a statute what it means and means in a statute what it says there. When the words of a statute are unambiguous, then, this first canon is also the last: <judicial inquiry is complete.'"[12] The Court takes much the same approach when it chooses congressional intent rather than statutory text as its touchstone: a canon of construction should not be followed "when application would be tantamount to a formalistic disregard of congressional intent."[13]

Canons of construction are basically context-dependent "rules of thumb." That is to say, canons are general principles, many of them of the common-sense variety, for drawing inferences about the meaning of language. Since language derives much of its meaning from context, canons should not be treated as rules of law, but rather as "axioms of experience" that do "not preclude consideration of persuasive [contrary] evidence if it exists."[14] Context can provide that contrary evidence. Many of the difficulties that have been identified with reliance on canons of construction can be avoided if their importance is not overemphasized — if they are considered tools rather than "rules."

There are so many "canons" that there is apparent conflict among some of them. A 1950 article by Professor Karl Llewellyn attempted to demonstrate that many canons can be countered by equally correct but opposing canons.[15] The case was somewhat strained, since in some instances Llewellyn relied on statements in court opinions that were not so generally accepted as to constitute "canons." Nonetheless, the clear implication was that canons are useless because judges may pick and choose among them to achieve whatever result is desired. The Supreme Court had to deal with such a conflict in ruling on the retroactive effect of the Civil Rights Act of 1991; there were "seemingly contradictory statements" in earlier decisions declaring general principles that, on the one hand, "a court is to apply the law in effect at the time it renders its decision," and, on the other hand, that "retroactivity is not favored in the law."[16] The Court explained that these two principles were really not inconsistent, and held that the provisions at issue were not retroactive.[17] But even for those canons that do have equal opposites, a review of the Supreme Court's usages can reveal the preferences of the Justices in choosing between the opposites, and may prove helpful during congressional debate on legislation in the many instances in which issues of clarity and meaning are raised.

ORDINARY AND SPECIALIZED MEANING

Terms of Art

When the meaning of specific statutory language is at issue, courts often need to consider the meaning of particular words or phrases. If the word or phrase is defined in the statute (federal statutes frequently collect definitions in a "definitions" section), or elsewhere in the United States Code,[18] then that definition governs if applicable in the context used.[19] Even if the word or phrase is not defined by statute, it may have an accepted meaning in the area of law addressed by the statute,[20] it may have been borrowed from another statute under which it had an accepted meaning,[21] or it may have had an accepted and specialized meaning at common law.22 In each of these situations the accepted meaning governs[23] and the word or phrase is considered a technical term or "term of art." Justice Jackson explained why this reliance is appropriate:[24]

[W]here Congress borrows terms of art in which are accumulated the legal tradition and meaning of centuries of practice, it presumably knows and adopts the cluster of ideas that were attached to each borrowed word in the body of learning from which it was taken and the meaning its use will convey to the judicial mind unless otherwise instructed. In such a case, absence of contrary direction may be taken as satisfaction with widely accepted definitions, not as departure from them.

Ordinary Meaning and Dictionary Definitions

Words that are not terms of art and that are not statutorily defined are customarily given their ordinary meanings, often derived from the dictionary.[25] Thus, the Court has relied on regular dictionary definitions to interpret the word "marketing" as used in the Plant Variety Protection Act,26 and the word "principal" as used to modify a taxpayer's place of business for purposes of an income tax deduction,[27] and relied on Black's Law Dictionary for the more specialized meaning of the word "cognizable" as used in the Federal Tort Claims Act to identify certain causes of action.[28]

Of course application of dictionary definitions is not always a clear course; many words have several alternative meanings, and context must guide choice among them.[29] "Ambiguity is a creature not of definitional possibilities but of statutory context."[30] Witness the Supreme Court's conclusion that "use" of a firearm in commission of a drug offense or crime of violence includes trading a gun for drugs.[31] And sometimes dictionary meanings can cause confusion even if there are not multiple choices. As Judge Learned Hand observed, "it is one of the surest indexes of a mature and developed jurisprudence not to make a fortress out of the dictionary; but to remember that statutes always have some purpose or object to accomplish, whose sympathetic and imaginative discovery is the surest guide to their meaning."[32]

And/Or

Similar principles govern use of the words "and" and "or." Ordinarily, as in everyday English, use of the conjunctive "and" in a list means that all of the listed requirements must be satisfied,[33] while use of the disjunctive "or" means that only one of the listed requirements need be satisfied.[34] Courts do not apply these meanings "inexorably," however; if a "strict grammatical construction" will frustrate evident legislative intent, a court may read "and" as "or," or "or" as "and."[35] Moreover, statutory context can render the distinction secondary.[36]

Definite/Indefinite Article

As in common usage, a drafter's choice between the definite and indefinite article can affect meaning. "The definite article 'the' particularizes the subject which it precedes. It is a word of limitation as opposed to the indefinite or generalizing force of 'a' or 'an.'"[37]

Shall/May

Use of "shall" and "may" in statutes also mirrors common usage; ordinarily "shall" is mandatory and "may" is permissive.[38] These words[39] must be read in their broader statutory context, however, the issue often being whether the statutory directive itself is mandatory or permissive.[40] Use of both words in the same provision can underscore their different meanings,[41] and often the context will confirm that the ordinary meaning of one or the other was intended.[42] Occasionally, however, context will trump ordinary meaning.[43]

Singular/Plural

An elementary rule of statutory construction is that the singular includes the plural, and vice-versa.[44] Thus, a statutory directive that the Secretary of Transportation require automakers to install a warning system in new cars to alert drivers "when a tire is significantly under-inflated" is not satisfied by a system that fails to warn when two tires on the same side, or all four tires, are significantly underinflated.[45]

GENERAL, SPECIFIC, AND ASSOCIATED WORDS

Ordinarily, the specific terms of a statute override the general terms. "However inclusive may be the general language of a statute, it will not be held to apply to a matter specifically dealt with in another part of the same enactment."[46] As with other canons, context can dictate a contrary result.[47]

Another interpretational guide used from time to time is the principle noscitur a sociis, that "words grouped in a list should be given related meaning."[48] A corollary, ejusdem generis, instructs that, "where general words follow an enumeration of specific items, the general words are read as applying only to other items akin to those specifically enumerated."[49] These principles are probably honored more in the breach than in the acceptance, however. The Court explained on one occasion that they are only "instrumentalit[ies] for ascertaining the correct meaning of words when there is uncertainty."[50] A less charitable assessment is that the maxims do not aid in ascertaining meaning or deciding cases, but rather serve only to "classify and label results reached by other means."[51]

GRAMMATICAL RULES, PUNCTUATION

The old rule, borrowed from English law, was that "[p]unctuation is no part of the statute," and that "[c]ourts will . . . disregard the punctuation, or repunctuate, if need be, to render the true meaning of the statute."[52] The modern Court recognizes that grammar and punctuation often clarify meaning, and that skilled drafters can be expected to apply good grammar.[53] The Court has also found plain meaning resulting from verb tense.[54]

The Court remains reluctant, however, to place primary importance on punctuation. "A statute's plain meaning must be enforced . . . , and the meaning of a statute will typically heed the commands of its punctuation."[55] So said the Court — not, however, in applying a plain meaning consistent with punctuation, but instead while justifying a departure from that meaning. The Court went on to explain that "a purported plain meaning analysis based only on punctuation is necessarily incomplete and runs the risk of distorting a statute's true meaning."[56] "Overwhelming evidence from the structure, language, and subject matter" of the law led the Court to conclude that "in this unusual case" the punctuation at issue was the result of "a simple scrivener's error."[57] While the Court has relied on comma placement to find that a plain meaning was "mandated by the grammatical structure of the statute," the Court in that case also found other support for its reading.[58]

Perhaps more typical was the Court's refusal to apply the rule that a modifying clause modifies the last antecedent, even though it could easily have concluded on the basis of the statutory language that application of the last antecedent rule was "mandated by the [statute's] grammatical structure." The rule "is quite sensible as a matter of grammar," the Court explained, but it "is not compelled."[59] So too, in another case the Court shied away from "the most natural grammatical reading" of a statute in order to avoid an interpretation that would have raised a serious issue of constitutionality.[60]

Refusal to be bound by the rules of punctuation and grammar, it seems, gives the Court some flexibility in construing statutes. This is not to say, however, that grammatical rules should be disregarded in statutory drafting, since such rules are ordinarily strong guides to meaning.

STATUTORY LANGUAGE NOT TO BE CONSTRUED AS "MERE SURPLUSAGE"

A basic principle of statutory interpretation is that courts should "give effect, if possible, to every clause and word of a statute, avoiding, if it may be, any construction which implies that the legislature was ignorant of the meaning of the language it employed."[61] The modern variant is that statutes should be construed "so as to avoid rendering superfluous" any statutory language.[62] A related principle applies to statutory amendments: there is a "general presumption" that, "when Congress alters the words of a statute, it must intend to change the statute's meaning."[63] Resistance to treating statutory words as mere surplusage "should be heightened when the words describe an element of a criminal offense."[64] There can be differences of opinion, of course, as to when it is "possible" to give effect to all statutory language and when the general rule should give way in the face of evident contrary meaning. [65]

A converse of the rule that courts should not read statutory language as surplusage is that courts should not add language that Congress has not included. Thus, in a situation where Congress subjected specific categories of ticket sales to taxation but failed to cover another category, either by specific or by general language, the Court refused to extend the coverage. To do so, given the "particularization and detail" with which Congress had set out the categories, would amount to "enlargement" of the statute rather than "construction" of it.[66]

SAME PHRASING IN SAME OR RELATED STATUTES

"A term appearing in several places in a statutory text is generally read the same way each time it appears."[67] This presumption is "at its most vigorous when a term is repeated within a given sentence."[68] The general presumption is not rigid, however, and "readily yields when there is such variation in the connection in which the words are used as reasonably to warrant the conclusion that they were employed in different parts of the act with different intent."[69] In other words, context can override the presumption.

DIFFERENT PHRASINGS IN SAME STATUTE

The other side of the coin is that "where Congress includes particular language in one section of a statute but omits it in another . . . , it is generally presumed that Congress acts intentionally and purposely in the disparate inclusion or exclusion."[70] "[N]egative implications raised by disparate provisions are strongest when the portions of a statute treated differently had already been joined together and were being considered simultaneously when the language raising the implication was inserted."[71] This maxim has been applied by the Court — or at least cited as a justification — in distinguishing among different categories of veterans benefits [72] and among different categories of drug offenses.[73] A court can only go so far with the maxim, of course; establishing that language does not mean one thing does not necessarily establish what the language does mean.[74]

"CONGRESS KNOWS HOW TO SAY ... "

Occasionally the Court draws a contrast between the language at issue and other statutory language that clearly and directly requires the interpretation being pressed by one of the parties. There are some instances — e.g., failure to employ terms of art or other language normally used for such purposes — in which this can be a fairly persuasive argument. For example, the Court reasoned that, although "Congress knew how to impose aiding and abetting liability when it chose to do so," it did not use the words "aid" and "abet" in the statute, and hence did not impose aiding and abetting liability.[75] To say that Congress did not use the clearest language, however, does not necessarily aid the court in determining what the less precise language means in its statutory context.[76] Some statutes are not well drafted,[77] and others represent conscious choices, born of political compromise, to leave issues for the courts to resolve.[78] It may not always be safe to assume, therefore, that "[i]f Congress had intended such an irrational result, surely it would have expressed it in straightforward English."[79]

STATUTORY SILENCE

Nor is it safe to assume that Congress can or will address directly and explicitly all issues that may arise. "As one court has aptly put it, '[n]ot every silence is pregnant.' In some cases, Congress intends silence to rule out a particular statutory application, while in others Congress' silence signifies merely an expectation that nothing more need be said in order to effectuate the relevant legislative objective. In still other instances, silence may reflect the fact that Congress has not considered an issue at all. An inference drawn from congressional silence certainly cannot be credited when it is contrary to all other textual and contextual evidence of congressional intent."[80] Occasionally, however, the Court identifies a pregnant statutory silence, as, for example, when that silence contrasts with a consistent pattern in federal statutes under which departures from a general rule had been expressly authorized.[81]

While Congress cannot be expected to anticipate and address all issues that may arise, the Court does sometimes assume that Congress will address major issues, at least in the context of amendment. "Congress . . . does not alter the fundamental details of a regulatory scheme in vague terms or ancillary provisions — it does not . . . hide elephants in mouseholes."[82] This premise underlay the Court's reasoning in concluding that the FDA lacked authority to regulate tobacco. "Congress could not have intended to delegate a decision of such economic and political significance to an agency in so cryptic a fashion."[83]

A variation on the statutory silence theme is the negative inference: expressio unius est exclusio alterius (the inclusion of one is the exclusion of others). "Where Congress explicitly enumerates certain exceptions to a general prohibition, additional exceptions are not to be implied, in the absence of a contrary legislative intent."[84] The Court applied the principle, albeit without express recognition, in holding that a statute requiring payment of an attendance fee to "a witness" applies to an incarcerated state prisoner who testifies at a federal trial. Because Congress had expressly excepted another category (detained aliens) from eligibility for these fees, and had expressly excepted any "incarcerated" witness from eligibility for a different category of fees, "the conclusion is virtually inescapable . . . that the general language 'witness in attendance' . . . includes prisoners . . . ."[85] But here again, context may render the principle inapplicable. A statutory listing may be "exemplary, not exclusive," the Court once concluded.[86]

DE MINIMIS PRINCIPLE

"The venerable maxim de minimis non curat lex ('the law cares not for trifles') is part of the established background of legal principles against which all enactments are adopted, and which all enactments (absent contrary indication) are deemed to accept. . . . Whether a particular activity is a de minimis deviation from a prescribed standard must . . . be determined with reference to the purpose of the standard."[87]

Chapter 3

OVERRIDING PRESUMPTIONS

There are a number of instances in which the Court stacks the deck, and subordinates the general, linguistic canons of statutory construction, as well as other interpretive principles, to overriding presumptions that favor particular substantive results. Some of the "weighty and constant values" protected by these presumptions are derived from the Constitution, and some are not.[88] Application of a presumption results in some form of "clear statement" rule, requiring that Congress, if it wishes to achieve a particular result inconsistent with the Court's view of legal traditions, must state such an intent with unmistakable clarity.[89] Legislative drafters need to be especially careful whenever overriding presumptions may be implicated. To that end, a number are briefly described below.

DEPARTURE FROM COMMON LAW OR ESTABLISHED INTERPRETATION

There is a presumption favoring continuation of judge-made law. "The normal rule of statutory construction is that if Congress intends for legislation to change the interpretation of a judicially created concept, it makes that intent specific."[90] In another case the Court declared that "[w]e will not read the Bankruptcy Code to erode past bankruptcy practice absent a clear indication that Congress intended such a departure."[91] This principle is thus closely akin to the principle noted above that, when Congress employs legal terms of art, it normally adopts the meanings associated with those terms.

DISPLACING STATE LAW, IMPINGING ON STATE OPERATIONS

The Supremacy Clause of the Constitution, Article VI, cl. 2, provides that valid federal law supersedes inconsistent state law. Courts encounter difficulty in applying this simple principle, however, especially when federal law is silent as to preemptive effect. The Court usually begins preemption analysis "with the assumption that the historic police powers of the States were not to be superseded by [a federal law] unless that was the clear and manifest purpose of Congress."[92] If the statute in question contains an explicit statement of preemptive scope, therefore, either preempting state law or disclaiming intent to do so, that is usually the end of the matter.[93] The Court also, however, recognizes several categories of implied preemption of state law, various formulations of which are that state law must give way to federal law if there is a direct conflict between them, if implementation of state law would "frustrate congressional purpose," or if federal law has "occupied the field" of regulation. These latter two categories lack precision, and, almost always, the surer course of legislative drafting is to spell out intended preemptive effect.

In the same vein, the Court will not lightly infer that Congress has enacted legislation that restricts how states may constitute their own governments. In ruling that state judges are not "employees" for purposes of the Age Discrimination in Employment Act, the Court required a plain statement rule applicable to laws limiting the authority of the States to determine the qualifications of their most important government officials — an authority protected by the Tenth Amendment and by the Guarantee Clause.[94] "This plain statement rule is nothing more than an acknowledgment that the States retain substantial sovereign powers under our constitutional scheme, powers with which Congress does not readily interfere."[95]

ABROGATION OF STATES' ELEVENTH AMENDMENT IMMUNITY

Also protective of state sovereignty is the rule that, in order to abrogate the states' Eleventh Amendment immunity from suit in federal court, "Congress must make its intention 'unmistakably clear in the language of the statute.'"[96] Congress, of course, has limited authority to abrogate states' Eleventh Amendment immunity; the Court held in Seminole Tribe of Florida v. Florida, that Article I powers may not be used to "circumvent the constitutional limitations placed upon federal jurisdiction [by the Eleventh Amendment]."[97] This leaves Section 5 of the Fourteenth Amendment as the principal source of power to abrogate state immunity.

NATIONWIDE APPLICATION OF FEDERAL LAW

Congress may, if it chooses, incorporate state law as federal law.[98] Federal law usually applies uniformly nationwide,[99] however, and there is a presumption that, "when Congress enacts a statute . . . it does not intend to make its application dependent on state law."[100]

WAIVER OF SOVEREIGN IMMUNITY

"[T]he Government's consent to be sued 'must be construed strictly in favor of the sovereign.'"101 Waiver of sovereign immunity must be effected by unequivocal expression in the statutory text itself; legislative history "has no bearing" on the issue.102 As a consequence, "statutes which in general terms divest pre-existing rights or privileges will not be applied to the sovereign without express words to that effect."[103]

NON-RETROACTIVITY / EFFECTIVE DATE

"[A]bsent a clear direction by Congress to the contrary, a law takes effect on the date of its enactment."[104] There is a general rule, based on the unfairness of attaching new legal consequences to already-completed events, disfavoring retroactive application of civil statutes. Statutory provisions do not apply to events antedating enactment unless there is clear congressional intent that they so apply. "Requiring clear intent assures that Congress itself has affirmatively considered the potential unfairness of retroactive application and determined that it is an acceptable price to pay for the countervailing benefits."105 The prohibitions on ex post facto laws, of course, impose a constitutional bar to retroactive application of penal laws.[106].

AVOIDANCE OF CONSTITUTIONAL ISSUES

The doctrine of "constitutional doubt" requires courts to construe statutes, "if fairly possible, so as to avoid not only the conclusion that it is unconstitutional but also grave doubts upon that score."[107] "[W]here an otherwise acceptable construction of a statute would raise serious constitutional problems, the Court will construe the statute to avoid such problems unless such construction is plainly contrary to the intent of Congress. . . . 'The elementary rule is that every reasonable construction must be resorted to, in order to save a statute from unconstitutionality.' This approach not only reflects the prudential concern that constitutional issues not be needlessly confronted, but also recognizes that Congress, like this Court, is bound by and swears an oath to uphold the Constitution."[108] "Grave doubt" as to constitutionality does not arise simply because a Court minority — even a minority of four Justices — believes a statute is unconstitutional; rather, a Court majority must "gravely . . . doubt that the statute is constitutional."[109]

EXTRATERRITORIAL APPLICATION DISFAVORED

"It is a longstanding principle of American law 'that legislation of Congress, unless a contrary intent appears, is meant to apply only within the territorial jurisdiction of the United States.' This 'canon of construction' . . . serves to protect against unintended clashes between our laws and those of other nations which could result in international discord."[110]

JUDICIAL REVIEW OF ADMINISTRATIVE ACTION

As a general matter, there is a "strong presumption that Congress intends judicial review of administrative action."[111] This presumption is embodied in the Administrative Procedure Act, which provides that "final agency action for which there is no other adequate remedy in a court [is] subject to judicial review."[112] The Administrative Procedure Act applies "except to the extent that . . . statutes preclude judicial review,"[113] and issues relating to application of the presumption usually arise in determining whether there is "clear and convincing evidence"[114] or "persuasive reason to believe"[115] that Congress intended to preclude judicial review. The presumption may be overcome by specific statutory language, but it also "may be overcome by inferences of intent drawn from the statutory scheme as a whole."[116]

DEFERENCE TO ADMINISTRATIVE INTERPRETATION

When a court reviews an agency's formal interpretation of a statute that the agency administers, and when the statute has not removed agency discretion by compelling a particular disposition of the matter at issue, courts defer to any reasonable agency interpretation. This is the Chevron rule announced in 1984.[117] In two decisions, one in 2000 [118] and one in 2001,[119] the Court clarified and narrowed Chevron's application, ruling that Chevron deference applies only if an agency's interpretation is the product of a formal agency process, such as adjudication or notice-and-comment rulemaking, through which Congress has authorized the agency "to speak with the force of law."[120] Other agency interpretations that are made without the protections of a formal and public process are reviewed under pre- Chevron principles set forth in Skidmore v. Swift & Co.[121]

If Chevron applies, the first question is "whether Congress has directly spoken to the precise question at issue."[122] If the court, "employing the traditional tools of statutory construction," determines that Congress has addressed the precise issue, then that is the end of the matter, because the "law must be given effect."[123] But if the statute does not directly address the issue, "the court does not simply impose its own construction of the statute," but rather determines "whether the agency's answer is based on a permissible construction of the statute."[124]

On its face, the Chevron rule is quite deferential, and was perceived as a significant break from the multi-factored approach that preceded it. One would expect that a court's conclusion as to whether Congress has "directly spoken" to the issue would be decisive in most cases, that most of the myriad of issues that can arise in the administrative setting would not be directly addressed by statute, and that, consequently, courts would most often defer to what are found to be "reasonable" agency interpretations.[125] Surprisingly, however, Chevron did not usher in an era of increased deference by the Supreme Court. The Court has frequently determined that in fact Congress has settled the matter, and that consequently there is no need to proceed to the second, more deferential step of the inquiry.[126] The Court has also found that, even though Congress has left the matter for agency resolution, the agency's interpretation is unreasonable.[127]

How the Court determines whether Congress has "directly addressed" an issue takes on critical importance. Chevron is not a strong "clear statement" rule, since the Court has considered legislative history as well as text in assessing the controlling weight of statute.[128] And even when relying solely on text, the Court has not adhered strictly to the original Chevron step-one formulation, sometimes instead employing a broad textualist approach that emphasizes "plain meaning" and abandons inquiry into whether Congress has addressed the "precise question" at issue.[129] This "plain meaning" alternative has the effect of expanding the circumstances under which the Court can resolve a case on statutory grounds rather than proceeding to stage two and deferring to an agency's interpretation.

The Court has recognized that there are some circumstances in which it is less likely that Congress intended to leave resolution of statutory ambiguity to the administering agency.[130] Thus, in holding that the FDA lacked authority to regulate tobacco products, the Court concluded that "Congress could not have intended to delegate a decision of such economic and political significance to an agency in so cryptic a fashion."[131] Rather than finding Chevron analysis inapplicable, however, the Court ruled that Congress had "directly spoken" to the regulatory issue — not through the FDCA itself, but rather through subsequently enacted tobacco-specific legislation and through rejection of legislative proposals to confer jurisdiction on the FDA.[132] In another case, the Court deemed deference to be inappropriate where the agency interpretation "invokes the outer limits of Congress' power," and there is no "clear indication" that Congress intended that result.[133]

A logical consequence of applying Chevron is to render irrelevant whether an agency interpretation was "contemporaneous" with a statute's enactment, or whether an agency's position has been consistent over the years. "Neither antiquity nor contemporaneity with the statute is a condition of validity."[134] The fact that an agency has changed its position over the years "is not fatal," because "the whole point of Chevron is to leave the discretion provided by the ambiguities of a statute with the implementing agency."[135]

The Supreme Court has also ruled in National Cable & Telecommunications Assn. v. Brand X Internet Services (Brand X) that a federal court must defer to a reasonable agency interpretation of an ambiguous statute even if, prior to the agency interpretation, the circuit has adopted a differing interpretation in an opinion.[136] The only time a prior judicial interpretation of a statute trumps an agency interpretation is when the federal court's interpretation flows from an unambiguous reading of the statute.[137]

Agency interpretations that take place in the many less formal contexts where Chevron deference is inapplicable (e.g., opinion letters, policy statements, agency manuals, and enforcement guidelines, "all of which lack the force of law"[138]) can still be "entitled to respect" under the Skidmore decision,[139] "but only to the extent that [they] have the power to persuade."[140] To make this determination, courts look to such factors as whether an interpretation dealt with technical and complex matters that fell within an area of agency expertise,[141] whether an agency's decision was wellreasoned,[142] whether the agency's interpretation was contemporaneous with the statute's enactment,[143] and whether the agency's interpretation was longstanding or consistent.[144]

REPEALS BY IMPLICATION

If Congress intends one statute to repeal an earlier statute or section of a statute in toto, it usually says so directly in the repealing act. There are other occasions when Congress intends one statute to supersede an earlier statute to the extent of conflict, but intends the earlier statute to remain in effect for other purposes. This too is often spelled out, usually in a section captioned "effect on existing law," "construction with other laws," or the like. "[It] can be strongly presumed that Congress will specifically address language on the statute books that it wishes to change."[145] Not infrequently, however, conflicts arise between the operation of two federal statutes that are silent as to their relationship. In such a case, courts will try to harmonize the two so that both can be given effect. A court "must read [two allegedly conflicting] statutes to give effect to each if [it] can do so while preserving their sense and purpose."[146] Only if provisions of two different federal statutes are "irreconcilably conflicting,"[147] or "if the later act covers the whole subject of the earlier one and is clearly intended as a substitute,"[148] will courts apply the rule that the later of the two prevails. "[R]epeals by implication are not favored, . . . and will not be found unless an intent to repeal is clear and manifest."[149] And in fact, the Court rarely finds repeal by implication.[150] As Judge Posner has pointed out, this canon is "a mixed bag. It protects some old statutes from . . . inadvertent destruction, but it threatens to impale new statutes on the concealed stakes planted by old ones."[151]

Laws of the Same Session

The presumption against implied repeals "is all the stronger" if both laws were passed by the same session of Congress.[152] But, in the case of an irreconcilable conflict between two laws of the same session, the later enactment will be deemed to have repealed the earlier one to the extent of the conflict.[153] Because the focus here is on legislative intent (or presumed legislative intent), time of legislative consideration, rather than effective dates of the statutes, is the key to determining which enactment was the "later" one.[154]

Appropriations Laws

The doctrine disfavoring repeals by implication also "applies with even greater force when the claimed repeal rests solely on an Appropriations Act," since it is presumed that appropriations laws do not normally change substantive law.[155] Nevertheless, Congress can repeal substantive law through appropriations measures if intent to do so is clearly expressed.[156]

RULE OF LENITY

The "rule of lenity" requires that "before a man can be punished as a criminal . . . his case must be plainly and unmistakably within the provisions of some statute."[157] Lenity principles "demand resolution of ambiguities in criminal statutes in favor of the defendant."[158] The reasons for the rule are that "'fair warning should be given to the world in language that the common world will understand, of what the law intends to do if a certain line is passed'" and that "'legislatures and not courts should define criminal activity.'"159 If statutory language is unambiguous, the rule of lenity is inapplicable.[160]

SCIENTER

Intent is generally a required element of a criminal offense, and consequently there is a presumption in favor of a scienter or mens rea requirement in a criminal statute. The presumption applies "to each of the statutory elements which criminalize otherwise innocent conduct."[161] The Court may read an express scienter requirement more broadly than syntax would require or normally permit,[162] and may read into a criminal prohibition a scienter requirement that is not expressed.[163] The Court recognizes some "strict liability" exceptions, especially for "public welfare" statutes regulating conduct that is inherently harmful or injurious and that is therefore unlikely to be perceived as lawful and innocent.[164] Determining whether such an exception applies can be difficult.[165] However, if the statute does not preclude a holding that scienter is required, and if the public welfare exception is deemed inapplicable, "far more than the simple omission of the appropriate phrase from the statutory definition is necessary to justify dispensing with an intent requirement."[166]

REMEDIAL STATUTES

One can search in vain for recent Supreme Court reliance on the canon that "remedial statutes" should be "liberally" or "broadly" construed.[167] This is probably due to a variety of factors, including recognition that the principle is difficult to apply and almost hopelessly general.[168] This is because many statutes are arguably "remedial," and consequently courts have wide discretion in determining scope of application. There may also be uncertainty over what "liberal" or "broad" construction means.[169] But if the principle is reformulated as merely requiring that ambiguities in a remedial statute be resolved in favor of persons for whose benefit the statute was enacted,[170] the principle should be no more difficult to apply (once a "remedial" statute has been identified) than the rule of lenity, which counsels resolution of ambiguities in penal statutes in favor of defendants.[171] Absence of this principle from the current Court's lexicon, therefore, may reflect substantive preferences of the Justices as well as recognition of its limitations. Then too, the Court may employ more specific or limited presumptions in circumstances in which earlier Courts might have cited the liberal-remedial maxim,[172] or may instead prefer in such circumstances to analyze a statute without reliance on canonical crutches. Categorizing a statute as "remedial," or even as a "civil rights statute," is no substitute for more refined analysis of the purposes of the particular statute at issue.[173]

STATUTES BENEFITTING INDIAN TRIBES

Another subcategory of the "remedial" statutes canon is the proposition that "statutes passed for the benefit of dependent Indian tribes . . . are to be liberally construed to favor Indians."[174] Most cases resolving issues relating to tribal matters implicate some variation of this proposition, [175] but frequently there are also statute- specific considerations that amplify [176] or outweigh [177] any such generalities.

MISCELLANY

TITLES OF ACTS OR SECTIONS

Although "it has long been established that the title of an Act 'cannot enlarge or confer powers,'"[178] the title of a statute or section "can aid in resolving an ambiguity in the legislation's text."[179] As Chief Justice Marshall explained, "[w]here the mind labours to discover the design of the legislature, it seizes everything from which aid can be derived."[180] A title or heading, however, being only "a short-hand reference to the general subject matter involved" and "not meant to take the place of the detailed provisions of the text,"[181] can provide only limited interpretive aid. Thus, a heading may shed light on the section's basic thrust,[182] or on ambiguous language in the text, but it "cannot limit the plain meaning of the text,"[183] and "has no power to give what the text of the statute takes away."[184]

PREAMBLES ("WHEREAS CLAUSES")

Preambles, or "whereas clauses," precede the enacted language, "are not part of the act," and consequently "cannot enlarge or confer powers, nor control the words of the act, unless they are doubtful or ambiguous."[185] Nonetheless, "whereas clauses" sometimes serve the same purpose as findings and purposes sections, and can provide useful insight into congressional concerns and objectives.[186] As with titles, preambles can sometimes help resolve ambiguity in enacted language.[187]

FINDINGS AND PURPOSES SECTIONS

In applying the general principle that statutory language should be interpreted in a manner consistent with statutory purpose, courts naturally look to the stated purposes of legislation in order to resolve ambiguities in the more specific language of operative sections. For example, the Court relied in part on the Racketeer Influenced and Corrupt Organizations (RICO) statute's broad purpose of seeking "the eradication of organized crime in the United States," to conclude that the term "enterprise" as used in the act includes criminal conspiracies organized solely for illegitimate purposes, and is not limited to legitimate businesses that are infiltrated by organized crime.[188]

It is easy, however, to place too much reliance on general statutory purposes in resolving narrow issues of statutory interpretation. Legislation seldom if ever authorizes each and every means that can be said to further a general purpose,189 and there is also the possibility that stated or inferred purposes may in some instances conflict with one another.[190]

"SENSE OF CONGRESS" PROVISIONS

"Sense of Congress" language is appropriate if Congress wishes to make a statement without making enforceable law. Ordinarily, a statement that it is the "sense of Congress" that something "should" be done is merely precatory, and creates no legal rights.[191] In the appropriate context "sense of Congress" language can have the same effect as statements of congressional purpose — that of resolving ambiguities in more specific language of operative sections of a law — but if that is the intent the more straightforward approach is to declare a "purpose" rather than a "sense."[192]

SAVINGS CLAUSES

Savings (or "saving") clauses are designed to preserve remedies under existing law. "The purpose of a savings clause is merely to nix an inference that the statute in which it appears is intended to be the exclusive remedy for harms caused by the violation of the statute."[193] A corollary is that a savings clause typically does not create a cause of action.[194]

Inclusion of a savings clause, however, does not make all pre-existing remedies compatible with the newly enacted law. If there is a conflict, the savings clause gives way.[195] Courts will attempt to give the savings language some effect, but may have to narrow that effect to avoid eviscerating the new law. A reference to specific remedies to be preserved can ease interpretation.[196] In some cases, the legislative history of the savings provision can reveal its purpose.[197] In other cases courts must reason from the scope and purpose of the new statute. For example, when the Carmack Amendment to the Interstate Commerce Act imposed comprehensive federal regulation governing the liability of interstate carriers, the Court held that savings language preserving "any remedy or right of action . . . under existing law" applied only to federal, not state remedies. To allow resort to state law remedies that were inconsistent with the federal regulation would negate the Amendment's effect. "[T]he act cannot be said to destroy itself," the Court concluded.[198] Even very clear savings language will not be allowed to thwart what the Court views as the objective of the federal enactment.[199]

"NOTWITHSTANDING ANY OTHER PROVISION OF LAW"

Congress sometimes underscores statutory directives by requiring that they be undertaken "notwithstanding any other provision of law." This phrase seldom aids interpretation. It is the statutory equivalent of a parent telling a child "I'm serious," or "I really mean it." Despite the admonition, courts and administrators still must determine what the underlying directive means. And, ordinarily, there will still be other provisions of law that apply; the trick is to determine which ones.[200] Courts have recognized these difficulties. One court, for example, ruled that a directive to proceed with offering and awarding of timber sale contracts "notwithstanding any other provision of law" meant only "notwithstanding any provision of environmental law," and did not relieve the Forest Service from complying with federal contracting law requirements governing such matters as non-discrimination, small business set- asides, and export restrictions.[201] "We have repeatedly held that the phrase 'notwithstanding any other law' is not always construed literally . . . and does not require the agency to disregard all otherwise applicable laws."[202] In the few instances in which the "notwithstanding" phrase may be marginally helpful to interpretation, it still must play second fiddle to a clear and unambiguous statement of the underlying directive,[203] and it is not as helpful as spelling out which other laws are to be disregarded.[204]

IMPLIED PRIVATE RIGHT OF ACTION

From time to time courts have held that a federal statute that does not explicitly create a private cause of action nonetheless implicitly creates one.[205] This notion traces to the old view that every right must have a remedy.[206] As the Supreme Court put it in an early implication case, where "disregard of the command of a statute . . . results in damage to one of the class for whose especial benefit the statute was enacted, the right to recover damages from the party in default is implied."[207] The Court has gradually retreated from that position,[208] and now is willing to find an implied private right of action only if it concludes that Congress intended to create one. This raises an obvious question: if Congress intended to create a cause of action, why did it not do so explicitly?[209] While the Court has attempted to explain that it does not mean actual intent,[210] the test now seems weighted against finding an implied private cause of action.[211] Legislative drafters wishing to create a private right of action should therefore do so explicitly.

INCORPORATION BY REFERENCE

Interpretational difficulties may also arise if one statute incorporates by reference provisions of an existing statute. A leading treatise declares that incorporations by "general reference" normally include subsequent amendments, but that incorporations by "specific reference" normally do not.[212] A general reference "refers to the law on the subject generally," while a specific reference "refers specifically to a particular statute by its title or section number."[213]

SEVERABILITY

When one section of a law is held unconstitutional, courts are faced with determining whether the remainder of the statute remains valid, or whether the whole statute is nullified. "Unless it is evident that the Legislature would not have enacted those provisions which are within its power, independently of that which is not, the invalid part may be dropped if what is left is fully operative as a law."[214] Congress frequently includes a pro forma severability clause in a statute,[215] and this reinforces a "presumption" of severability by removing much of the doubt about congressional intent.[216] A severability clause does not guarantee, however, that what remains of a statute after a portion has been invalidated is "fully operative"; courts sometimes find that valid portions of a statute cannot stand on their own even though Congress has included a severability clause.[217] Far less frequently, Congress includes nonseverability language providing that remaining sections of a law shall be null and void if a part (sometimes a specified part) is held unconstitutional.[218] Case law is sparse,[219] but there is no apparent reason why courts should refuse to honor a clearly expressed non-severability directive.[220]

DEADLINES FOR ADMINISTRATIVE ACTION

"If a statute does not specify a consequence for noncompliance with statutory timing provisions, the federal courts will not in the ordinary course impose their own coercive sanction."[221] Absent specified consequences, such deadlines "are at best precatory rather than mandatory,"[222] and are read "as a spur to prompt action, not as a bar to tardy completion."[223] "A statute directing official action needs more than a mandatory 'shall' before the grant of power can sensibly be read to expire when the job is supposed to be done."[224] Thus, agency actions taken after a deadline are ordinarily upheld as valid.[225] Although courts are loath to impose "coercive" sanctions that would defeat the purpose of the underlying agency duty, courts sometimes will lend their authority, backed by the possibility of contempt for recalcitrant agency officials, by ordering compliance with statutory directives after a missed deadline.[226]

Chapter 5

LEGISLATIVE HISTORY

PLAIN MEANING RULE

Although over the years the plain meaning rule, which purports to bar courts from relying on legislative history when statutory language is plain, may have been more honored in the breach than the observance,[227] that trend has reversed. And even when breached, the "rule" is usually paid lip service, and becomes the semantic bridge to a court's consideration of legislative history. That is to say, a court that actually relies on legislative history will usually do so only after expressing a belief that the statutory language is not plain, but instead is unclear or "ambiguous."[228]

Significant differences arise, however, in the willingness of courts to label particular statutory language as "ambiguous" and thereby legitimize resort to legislative history. Some judges are more confident than others in their ability to interpret statutory text, and some are more convinced than others of the propriety of attempting to do so without resort to the "extrinsic" aid of legislative history.[229] Correspondingly, there are basic differences in approach, from narrow focus on the clarity or ambiguity of the particular statutory phrase at issue, to recognition that phrases that may seem ambiguous in isolation may be clarified by statutory context. [230] And, inevitably, there are real differences in the clarity of statutory language.[231]

Agreement on the basic meaning of the plain meaning rule — if it occurs — does not guarantee agreement over the rule's application. There have been cases in which Justices of the Supreme Court have agreed that the statutory provision at issue is plain, but have split 5-4 over what that plain meaning is.[232] There are other cases in which strict application is simply ignored; courts, after concluding that the statutory language is plain, nonetheless look to legislative history, either to confirm that plain meaning,[233] or to refute arguments that a contrary interpretation was "intended."[234] The one generally recognized exception to the rule is that a plain meaning is rejected if it would produce an "absurd result."[235]

There is scholarly debate over the merits of the plain meaning rule.[236] There is probably general consensus, however, that the plain meaning rule aptly characterizes interpretational priorities (statutory language is primary, legislative history secondary), but that its usage often merely announces rather than determines results.

USES OF LEGISLATIVE HISTORY

Once a court has decided to look to legislative history, there is a question of how legislative history should be used. Possibilities range from background information about the general problems Congress sought to address in the legislation, to explanation of the specific statutory language at issue, to specific instructions about how to deal with the particular factual situation giving rise to the litigation. The first of these uses is generally considered legitimate, the second may or may not be, and the third is generally considered to be improper.

Reference to legislative history for background and historical context is commonplace. A "proper construction frequently requires consideration of [a statute's] wording against the background of its legislative history and in the light of the general objectives Congress sought to achieve."[237]

A distinct but related inquiry focuses not on the explanations that accompanied committee or floor consideration, but rather on the sequence of changes in bill language. Consideration of the "specific history of the legislative process that culminated in the [statute at issue] affords . . . solid ground for giving it appropriate meaning" and for resolving ambiguity present in statutory text.[238] Selection of one House's version over that of the other House may be significant.[239] In some circumstances rejection of an amendment can be important. While courts are naturally reluctant to attribute significance to the failure of Congress to act,[240] that reluctance may be overcome if it can be shown that Congress considered and rejected bill language that would have adopted the very position being urged upon the court.[241]

Explanatory legislative history is also consulted on occasion for more narrowly focused explanation of the meaning of specific statutory language that a court believes is unclear.[242] Reliance on legislative history for such purposes may be more controversial, either because contrary indications may be present in other passages of legislative history,[243] or because the degree of direction or detail may be an unwarranted narrowing of a more general statutory text.[244] The concern in the latter instances is whether the legislative history is a plausible explanation of language actually contained in the statutory text, or whether instead explanatory language (e.g., report language containing committee directives or "understandings") outpaces that text. As the Court observed in rejecting reliance on legislative history "excerpts" said to reflect congressional intent to preempt state law, "we have never [looked for] congressional intent in a vacuum, unrelated to the giving of meaning to an enacted statutory text. . . . [U]nenacted approvals, beliefs, and desires are not laws."[245]

Statutory silence is not always "pregnant,"[246] and silence of legislative history is seldom significant.[247] There is no requirement that "every permissible application of a statute be expressly referred to in its legislative history."[248] The Court does, however, occasionally attach import to the absence of any indication in a statute or its legislative history of an intent to effect a "major change" in well-established law.[249] And sometimes the Justices disagree over the significance of congressional silence.[250]

POST-ENACTMENT OR "SUBSEQUENT" LEGISLATIVE HISTORY

"The legislative history of a statute is the history of its consideration and enactment. 'Subsequent legislative history' — which presumably means the post-enactment history of a statute's consideration and enactment — is a contradiction in terms."[251] The Court frequently observes that "' [t]he views of a subsequent Congress form a hazardous basis for inferring the intent of an earlier one.'"[252] Actually, however, "post-enactment history" and "subsequent legislative history" are terms sometimes used as loose descriptions of several different kinds of congressional actions and inactions, and it is helpful to distinguish among them. The interpretational value — if any — of the views of a subsequent Congress depends upon how those views are expressed.

Subsequent Legislation

If the views of a later Congress are expressed in a duly enacted statute, then the views embodied in that statute must be interpreted and applied. Occasionally a later enactment declares congressional intent about interpretation of an earlier enactment rather than directly amending or clarifying the earlier law. Such action can be given prospective effect because, "however inartistic, it . . . stands on its own feet as a valid enactment."[253] "Subsequent legislation declaring the intent of an earlier statute is entitled to great weight in statutory construction."[254] Other statutes may be premised on a particular interpretation of an earlier statute; this interpretation may be given effect, especially if a contrary interpretation would render the amendments pointless or ineffectual.[255]

Reenactment

If Congress reenacts a statute and leaves unchanged a provision that had received a definitive administrative or judicial interpretation, the Court sometimes holds that Congress has ratified that interpretation.[256] The stated rationale is that "Congress is presumed to be aware of an administrative or judicial interpretation of a statute and to adopt that interpretation when it re-enacts a statute without change."[257] Similarly, if Congress in enacting a new statute incorporates sections of an earlier one, "Congress normally can be presumed to have had knowledge of the interpretation given to the incorporated law, at least insofar as it affects the new statute."[258] The reenactment presumption is usually indulged only if the history of enactment shows that Congress conducted a comprehensive review of the reenacted or incorporated statute, and changed those aspects deemed undesirable.[259] Note, however, that the presumption comes into play in the absence of direct evidence that Congress actually considered the issue at hand. Under these circumstances, other inferences as to the significance of congressional silence seem equally strong. Congress may have simply overlooked the matter, or may have intended to leave it "for authoritative resolution in the courts."[260]

Acquiescence

Congressional inaction is sometimes construed as approving or "acquiescing" in an administrative or judicial interpretation even if unaccompanied by the positive act of reenactment of the statute as a whole.[261] There is no general presumption that congressional inaction in the face of interpretation bespeaks acquiescence, and there is no consistent pattern of application by the Court. But when the Court does infer acquiescence, the most important factor (other than the

Court's agreement that the administrative or judicial interpretation is the correct one) seems to be congressional awareness that the interpretation has generated controversy.[262] As with reenactment, however, there are other inferences that can be drawn from congressional silence.[263]

"Isolated Statements"

Although congressional inaction or silence is sometimes accorded importance in interpreting an earlier enactment, post-enactment explanations or expressions of opinion by committees or members are often dismissed as "isolated statements" or "subsequent legislative history" not entitled to much if any weight. As the Court has noted, statements as to what a committee believes an earlier enactment meant are "obviously entitled to less weight" than is subsequent legislation declaring such intent, because in the case of the committee statement Congress had not "proceeded formally through the legislation process."[264] The Court has also explained that "isolated statements by individual Members of Congress or its committees, all made after enactment of the statute under consideration, cannot substitute for a clear expression of legislative intent at the time of enactment."[265] "It is the function of the courts and not the Legislature, much less a Committee of one House of the Legislature, to say what an enacted statute means."[266] The disfavor in which post-enactment explanations are held is sometimes expressed more strongly when the views are those of a single member. The Court has declared that "post hoc observations by a single member carry little if any weight."[267]

Chapter 6

SIGNING STATEMENTS

Judicial reliance on presidential signing statements to interpret statutes[268] poses problems above and beyond those presented by reliance on legislative materials, and there is no consensus as to whether courts should rely at all on signing statements.[269] Presidents' routine use of signing statements to try to influence statutory interpretation by courts is a relatively recent development,[270] there has been no definitive ruling by the Supreme Court, and even lower courts have seldom had to resolve cases that require a choice between conflicting presidential and congressional interpretations. Courts cite signing statements from time to time, but usually in situations where the interpretation is not critical to case outcome.[271]

The nature of the President's role in vetoing or approving legislation suggests that little interpretational weight should be given to signing statements. Article I, section 7, clause 2 of the U.S. Constitution provides that, after Congress passes a bill and presents it to the President, "if he approves he shall sign it, but if not he shall return it, with his Objections to that House in which it shall have originated, who shall enter the Objections at large on their Journal, and proceed to reconsider it." Several observations about this language are possible.

First, the President is required to set forth "objections" to a bill he vetoes, but there is no parallel requirement that he set forth his reasons for approving a bill. Correspondingly, there is a procedure for congressional consideration of the President's objections and for reconsideration of the bill following a veto, but no procedure for congressional response following a signing. Of course, absence of a constitutionally recognized procedure does not require that the President's views be discounted; after all, the Constitution is also silent about committee reports, floor debates, and other components of legislative history. But such absence does suggest that the President's views should be discounted when they conflict with congressional explanations otherwise entitled to weight. A rule for resolving conflicts in legislative history provides guidance here. When the two Houses have disagreed on the meaning of identical language in a bill that did not go to conference, the explanation that was before both Houses (i.e., the explanation of the originating House) prevails if the court relies on legislative history at all. The rationale is that congressional intent should depend upon the actions of both Houses. "By unanimously passing the Senate Bill without amendment, the House denied the entire Senate an opportunity to object (or concur) to [its] interpretation."[272] Similarly, because Congress has no opportunity to respond to interpretations set forth in signing statements, courts should not use those interpretations to change meaning.[273]

A second observation about the Constitutional text is that the President has a choice of approving or disapproving a "bill" in its entirety, and may not disapprove some portions while approving others. Not only does the President lack a line-item veto, but Congress can't grant the President such authority by statute.[274] Giving effect to a signing statement that would negate a statutory provision [275] can be considered analogous to a line item veto.[276]

The President's signing statement explanations of bill language may be entitled to more weight if the President or his Administration worked closely with Congress in developing the legislation, and if the approved version incorporated the President's recommendations.[277] This principle can be applied not only to bills introduced at the Administration's behest, but also to bills the final content of which resulted from compromise negotiations between the Administration and Congress.[278] In such circumstances, of course, signing statements are used to explain rather than negate congressional action, and are most valuable as lending support to congressional explanations.

Even if presidential signing statements should not be treated as a significant part of legislative history, they may still affect interpretation as directives to administering agencies. As explained above under "Deference to Administrative Interpretations,"[279] courts are highly deferential to interpretations of agencies charged with implementing statutes. Such deference, however, is premised on the conclusion that Congress has authorized the agency to "speak with the force of law" through a rulemaking or other formal process. Congress has not authorized the President to speak with the force of law through signing statements. So, although signing statements may influence or even control agency implementation of statutes, it is the implementation, and not the signing statement itself, that would be measured against the statute's requirements.[280] At most, signing statements might be considered analogous to informal agency actions, entitled to respect only to the extent that they have the power to persuade.[281]

REFERENCES

[1] This report was originally prepared by George Costello. It has now been updated by Yule Kim, who is available to answer questions on these issues.

[2] Finley v. United States, 490 U.S. 545, 556 (1989).

[3] 61 Fed. Reg. 4729 (February 5, 1996), reprinted in 28 U.S.C. § 519. The Order directs agencies to "make every reasonable effort to ensure" that proposed legislation, "as appropriate . . . specifies in clear language" — (A) whether causes of action arising under the law are subject to statutes of limitations; (B) the preemptive effect; (C) the effect on existing Federal law; (D) a clear legal standard for affected conduct; (E) whether arbitration and other forms of dispute resolution are appropriate; (F) whether the provisions of the law are severable if one or more is held unconstitutional; (G) the retroactive effect, if any; (H) the applicable burdens of proof; (I) whether private parties are granted a right to sue, and, if so, what relief is available and whether attorney's fees are available; (J) whether state courts have jurisdiction; (K) whether administrative remedies must be pursued prior to initiating court actions; (L) standards governing personal jurisdiction; (M) definitions of key statutory terms; (N) applicability to the Federal Government; (O) applicability to states, territories, the District of Columbia, and the Commonwealths of Puerto Rico and the Northern Mariana Islands; and (P) what remedies are available, "such as money damages, civil penalties, injunctive relief, and attorney's fees."

[4] It is because "'Congress is free to change this Court's interpretation of its legislation,'" that the Court adheres more strictly to the doctrine of stare decisis in the area of statutory construction than in the area of constitutional interpretation, where amendment is much more difficult. Neal v. United States, 516 U.S. 284, 295 (1996) (quoting Illinois Brick Co. v. Illinois, 431

U.S. 720, 736 (1977)); Shepard v. United States, 544 U.S. 13, 23 (2005). "Stare decisis is usually the wise policy [for statutes], because in most matters it is more important that the applicable rule of law be settled than that it be settled right." Burnet v. Coronado Oil & Gas Co., 285 U.S. 393, 406 (1932) (Justice Brandeis, dissenting).

[5]   One scholar identified 187 override statutes from 1967 to 1990. William N. Eskridge,
       Overriding Supreme Court Statutory Interpretation Decisions, 101 YALE L.J. 331 (1991).

[6]   See discussion of rule under "Legislative History," infra p. 39.

[7]   United Savings Ass'n v. Timbers of Inwood Forest Associates, 484 U.S. 365, 371 (1988) (citations omitted).

[8]   United States v. Boisdoré's Heirs, 49 U.S. (8 How.) 113, 122 (1850) (opinion of Court). For a modern instance in which the Court's reading of text was informed by statutory context and statutory purpose, see Brotherhood of Locomotove Engineers v. Atchison, T. & S.F.R.R., 516 U.S. 152, 157 (1996) (purpose of Hours of Service Act of promoting safety by ensuring that fatigued employees do not operate trains guides the determination of whether employees' time is "on duty"). As Justice Breyer explained, dissenting in FCC v. NextWave Personal Communications, Inc., 537 U.S. 293, 311 (2003), "[i]t is dangerous . . . in any case of interpretive difficulty to rely exclusively upon the literal meaning of a statute's words divorced from consideration of the statute's purpose." The Justice cited the stock example that "'no vehicles in the park' does not refer to baby strollers or even to tanks used as part of a war memorial," as well as Justice Field's opinion for the Court in United States v. Kirby, 74 U.S. (7 Wall.) 482, 486 (1869) (prohibition on obstructing mail does not apply to local sheriff's arrest of mail carrier on a murder charge; "[g]eneral terms should be so limited in their application as not to lead to injustice, oppression, or an absurd consequence").

[9]   Green v. Bock Laundry Machine Co., 490 U.S. 504, 528 (1990).

[10]   McNary v. Haitian Refugee Center, 498 U.S. 479, 496 (1991) (referring to presumption favoring judicial review of administrative action). See also United States v. Fausto, 484 U.S. 439, 463 n.9 (1988) (Justice Stevens, dissenting) (Court presumes that "Congress is aware of this longstanding presumption [disfavoring repeals by implication] and that Congress relies on it in drafting legislation").

[11]   SEC v. Joiner, 320 U.S. 344, 350-51 (1943). Justice Jackson explained that some of the canons derived "from sources that were hostile toward the

legislative process itself," and that viewed legislation as "'interference'" with the common law "'process of intelligent judicial administration.'" 320 U.S. at 350 & n.7 (quoting the first edition of SUTHERLAND, STATUTES AND STATUTORY CONSTRUCTION). A more recent instance of congressional purpose and statutory context trumping a "canon" occurred in General Dynamics Land Systems, Inc. v. Cline, 540 U.S. 581, 594-599 (2004), the Court determining that the word "age" is used in different senses in different parts of the Age Discrimination in Employment Act, and that consequently the presumption of uniform usage throughout a statute should not be followed.

[12] Connecticut Nat'l Bank v. Germain, 503 U.S. 249, 253-54 (1992) (citations omitted).

[13] Rice v. Rehner, 463 U.S. 713, 732 (1983).

[14] Boston Sand & Gravel Co. v. United States, 278 U.S. 41, 48 (1928) (Justice Holmes for Court).

[15] Karl Llewellyn, Remarks on the Theory of Appellate Decision and the Rules or Canons About How Statutes Are To Be Construed, 3 VAND. L. REV. 395 (1950).

[16] Landgraf v. USI Film Products, 511 U.S. 244, 263-64 (1994).

[17] Id.

[18] The Dictionary Act, ch. 388, 61 Stat. 633 (1947), as amended, 1 U.S.C. §§ 1-6, has definitions of a few common terms used in federal statutes (e.g., "person," "vessel," and "vehicle"). These definitions govern in all federal statutes "unless the context indicates otherwise." See Stewart v. Dutra Constr. Co., 543 U.S. 481, 489 (2005) (relying on Dictionary Act's definition of "vessel"); Rowland v. California Men's Colony, 506 U.S. 194 (1993) (context indicates otherwise; the term "person" as used in 28 U.S.C. § 1915(a) refers only to individuals and does not carry its Dictionary Act definition , which includes associations and artificial entities).

[19] Colautti v. Franklin, 439 U.S. 379, 392 (1979). If the context indicates otherwise, i.e., if a mechanical application of a statutory definition throughout a statute would create an "obvious incongruity" or frustrate an evident statutory purpose for a particular provision, then it is permissible to depart from the definition. Lawson v. Suwannee S.S. Co., 336 U.S. 198, 201 (1949). But, as noted below, a term appearing in several places in a statute is ordinarily interpreted as having the same meaning each time it appears. See section on "Same Phrasing in Same or Related Statutes," infra p. 13.

[20] See, e.g., Sullivan v. Stroop, 496 U.S. 478, 483 (1990) (phrase "child support" as used in Title IV AFDC provisions of Social Security Act). Note

also that "where a phrase in a statute appears to have become a term of art . . . , any attempt to break down the term into its constituent words is not apt to illuminate its meaning." Id.

[21]   In appropriate circumstances, courts will assume that "adoption of the wording of a statute from another legislative jurisdiction carries with it the previous judicial interpretations of the wording." Carolene Products Co. v. United States, 323 U.S. 18, 26 (1944) (finding, however, that circumstances were inappropriate for reliance on the principle). For the presumption to operate, the previous judicial interpretations must have been "known and settled." Capital Traction Co. v. Hof, 174 U.S. 1, 36 (1899). See also Yates v. United States, 354 U.S. 298, 310 (1957) (in the absence of legislative history indicating that decisions of lower state courts were called to Congress' attention, Court "should not assume that Congress was aware of them"). Variations in statutory wording may also refute the suggestion that Congress borrowed an interpretation. Shannon v. United States, 512 U.S. 573, 581 (1994) (Congress did not borrow the terms of the Insanity Defense Reform Act of 1984 from the District of Columbia Code).

[22]   See, e.g., Community for Creative Non-Violence v. Reid, 490 U.S. 730, 739-40 (1989) (relying on traditional common law agency principles for meaning of term "employee" as used without definition in the Copyright Act). See also Nationwide Mut. Ins. Co. v. Darden, 503 U.S. 318, 323 (1992) (following the same course after finding ERISA's "circular" definition of "employee" to be useless); Clackamas Gastroenterology Assocs., P.C. v. Wells, 538 U.S. 440, 444 (2003) (same construction of similarly "circular" definition of "employee" in ADA).

[23]   "[W]here a common law principle is well established, . . . the courts may take it as a given that Congress has legislated with an expectation that the principle will apply except 'when a statutory purpose to the contrary is evident.'" Astoria Federal Savings & Loan Ass'n v. Solimino, 501 U.S. 104, 108 (1991) (quoting Isbrandtsen Co. v. Johnson, 343 U.S. 779, 783 (1952)). No clear statement rule is required, however, in order to establish an "evident" contrary purpose. 501 U.S. at 108.

[24]   Morissette v. United States, 342 U.S. 246, 263 (1952). See also Miles v. Apex Marine Corp., 498 U.S. 19, 32 (1990) ("We assume that Congress is aware of existing law when it passes legislation").

[25]   In the absence of a statutory definition, "we construe a statutory term in accordance with its ordinary or natural meaning." FDIC v. Meyer, 510 U.S. 471, 476 (1994).

[26]   Asgrow Seed Co. v. Winterboer, 513 U.S. 179, 187 (1995).

[27] Commissioner v. Soliman, 506 U.S. 168, 174 (1993).

[28] FDIC v. Meyer, 510 U.S. 471, 476 (1994).

[29] See, e.g., MCI Tel. Corp. v. American Tel. & Tel. Co., 512 U.S. 218, 226-
      28 (1994) (FCC's authority to "modify" requirements does not include the
      authority to make tariff filing optional; aberrant dictionary meaning "to
      make a basic or important change" is antithetical to the principal meaning of
      incremental change and is more than the statute can bear); and Nixon v.
      Missouri Municipal League, 541 U.S. 125 (2004) (preemption of state laws
      that prohibit "any entity" from providing telecommunications service
      means, in context, "any private entity," and does not preempt a state law
      prohibiting local governments from providing such services). If the court
      views the issue as one of deference to an administrative interpretation, then
      the agency's choice of one alternative dictionary definition over another
      may indicate sufficient "reasonableness." Smiley v. Citibank (South
      Dakota), 517 U.S. 735, 744-47 (1996).

[30] Brown v. Gardner, 513 U.S. 115, 118 (1994).

[31] Smith v. United States, 508 U.S. 223 (1993). Dissenting Justice Scalia cut to
      the core: "[to] use an instrumentality normally means to use it for its
      intended purpose. When someone asks 'Do you use a cane?' he is not
      inquiring whether you have your grandfather's silver-handled walking-stick
      on display in the hall; he wants to know whether you walk with a cane.
      Similarly, to speak of 'using a firearm' is to speak of using it for its
      distinctive purpose, i.e., as a weapon." Id. at 242. The Court had less
      difficulty with the provision in 1995, overruling a lower court's holding that
      proximity and accessibility of a firearm are alone sufficient to establish
      "use." Bailey v. United States, 516 U.S. 137 (1995) (driving car with gun
      located in bag in car's trunk does not constitute "use" of gun; person who
      sold drugs after retrieving them from room in which gun was found in a
      locked trunk in a closet did not "use" that gun in sale). The Bailey Court,
      however, defined "use" in such a way ("active employment") as to leave the
      Smith holding intact. See also Muscarello v. United States, 524 U.S. 125
      (1998) (the companion phrase "carries a firearm," found in the same
      statutory provision, is a broader category that includes transporting drugs
      with a handgun locked in the glove compartment of a vehicle).

[32] Cabell v. Markham, 148 F.2d 737, 739 (2d Cir. 1945). Justice Stevens has
      expressed a preference for established interpretation over dictionary
      definitions. "In a contest between the dictionary and the doctrine of stare
      decisis, the latter clearly wins." Hibbs v. Winn, 542 U.S. 88, 113 (2004) (J.
      Stevens, concurring).

[33] See, e.g., Pueblo of Santa Ana v. Kelly, 932 F. Supp. 1284, 1292 (D. N. Mex. 1996).

[34] See, e.g., Zorich v. Long Beach Fire and Ambulance Serv., 118 F.3d 682, 684 (9th Cir. 1997); United States v. O'Driscoll, 761 F.2d 589, 597-98 (10th Cir. 1985). A corollary is that use of the disjunctive "or" creates "mutually exclusive"conditions that can rule out mixing and matching. United States v. Williams, 326 F.3d 535, 541 (4th Cir. 2003) ("a crime may qualify as a serious drug offense by meeting all the requirements of (i) or all the requirements of (ii), but not some of the requirements of (i) and some of (ii)").

[35] See, e.g., United States v. Moore, 613 F.2d 1029 (D.C. Cir. 1979); De Sylva v. Ballentine, 351 U.S. 570, 573 (1956) ("the word 'or' is often used as a careless substitute for the word 'and'"). Both "and" and "or" are context-dependent, and each word "is itself semantically ambiguous, and can be used in two quite different senses." LAWRENCE E. FILSON, THE LEGISLATIVE DRAFTER'S DESK REFERENCE, § 21.10 (1992).

[36] See, e.g., United States v. 14 1st St. Corp., 911 F.2d 870 (2d Cir. 1990) (holding that an affirmative defense to forfeiture of real property used in a drug offense, applicable if the offense was committed "without the knowledge or consent" of the property owner, applies if the property owner had knowledge of the crime, did not consent, and took all reasonable steps to prevent illicit use of his property).

[37] American Bus Ass'n v. Slater, 231 F.3d 1, 4-5 (D.C. Cir. 2000). See also Reid v. Angelone, 36. 9 F.3d 363, 367 (4th Cir. 2004) ("because Congress used the definite article 'the,' we conclude that . . . there is only one order subject to the requirements"); Warner- Lambert Corp. v. Apotex Corp., 316 F.3d 1348, 1356 (Fed. Cir. 2003) (reference to "the" use of a drug is a reference to an FDA-approved use, not to "a" use or "any" use); Freytag v. Commissioner, 501 U.S. 868, 902 (1991) (concurring opinion of Justice Scalia) (contending that use of the definite article in the Constitution's conferral of appointment authority on "the Courts of Law" "obviously narrows the class of eligible 'Courts of Law' to those courts of law envisioned by the Constitution"). But cf. Sprietsma v. Mercury Marine, 537 U.S. 51, 63 (2002) (reference in a preemption clause to "a law or regulation" "implies a discreteness — which is embodied in statutes and regulations — that is not present in the common law").

[38] "The mandatory 'shall' . . . normally creates an obligation impervious to judicial discretion." Lexecon, Inc. v. Milberg Weiss Bershad Hynes & Lerach, 523 U.S. 26, 35 (1998). "The use of a permissive verb — 'may

review' instead of 'shall review' — suggests a discretionary rather than mandatory review process." Rastelli v. Warden, Metro. Correctional Center, 782 F.2d 17, 23 (2d Cir. 1986).

[39] "Should" sometimes is substituted for "may" as a permissive word. Union Elec. Co. v. Consolidation Coal Co., 188 F.3d 998, 1001 (8th Cir. 1999). "Will" and "must" can be additional mandatory words. Bankers Ins. Co. v. Florida Res. Prop. & Cas. Jt. Underwriting Ass'n, 137 F.3d 1293, 1298 (11th Cir. 1998).

[40] See IA SUTHERLAND, STATUTES AND STATUTORY CONSTRUCTION § 25:4 (Norman J. Singer ed., 6th ed. 2002 rev.).

[41] See, e.g., Lopez v. Davis, 531 U.S. 230, 241 (2001) ("Congress' use of the permissive 'may' . . . contrasts with the legislators' use of a mandatory 'shall' in the very same section"); and United States ex rel. Siegel v. Thoman, 156 U.S. 353, 359-60 (1895) ("in the law to be construed here it is evident that the word 'may' is used in special contradistinction to the word 'shall'").

[42] See, e.g., Escoe v. Zerbst, 295 U.S. 490, 493 (1935) ("doubt . . . is dispelled when we pass from the words alone to a view of [the statute's] ends and aims").

[43] See, e.g., Moore v. Illinois Cent R.R., 312 U.S. 630, 635 (1941) (substitution of "may" for "shall" "was not, we think, an indication of a change in policy, but was instead a clarification of the [Railway Labor Act's] original purpose [of establishing] a system for peaceful adjustment and mediation voluntary in its nature"). See also discussion in Gutierrez de Martinez v. Lamagno, 515 U.S. 417, 432 n.9 (1995) ("shall" sometimes means "may").

[44] The Dictionary Act provides that "unless the context indicates otherwise," "words importing the singular include and apply to several persons, parties, or things; words importing the plural include the singular." 1 U.S.C. § 1.

[45] Public Citizen, Inc. v. Mineta, 340 F.3d 39, 54 (2d Cir. 2003).

[46] Fourco Glass Co. v. Transmirra Products Corp., 353 U.S. 222, 228 (1957) (citations omitted). The same principle is used to resolve conflict between two statutes. See, e.g., United States v. Estate of Romani, 523 U.S. 517, 532 (1998) (later, more specific statute governs). See also Morton v. Mancari, 417 U.S. 535, 550-51 (1974) (a general statute will not be held to have repealed by implication a more specific one unless there is "clear intention otherwise").

[47] See, e.g., Adams v. Woods, 6 U.S. (2 Cranch) 336, 341 (1805).

[48]   Dole v. United Steelworkers of America, 494 U.S. 26, 36 (1990); Gustafson
       v. Alloyd Co., 513 U.S. 561, 575 (1995) (reading a statutory definition as
       limited by the first of several grouped words).

[49]   Harrison v. PPG Industries, Inc., 446 U.S. 578, 588 (1980); Circuit City
       Stores, Inc. v. Adams, 532 U.S. 105, 114-15 (2001); Washington Dep't of
       Social Servs. v. Keffeler, 537 U.S. 371, 384 (2003) (relying on both
       noscitur a sociis and ejusdem generis). The principle cannot be applied if
       the enumerated categories are too "disparate." Arcadia v. Ohio Power Co.,
       498 U.S. 73, 78 (1990). And, of course, context may reveal that application
       is inappropriate. Norfolk & Western Ry. v. Train Dispatchers, 499 U.S. 117,
       129 (1991) (exemption of carriers from "the antitrust laws and all other law,
       including State and municipal law," is "clear, broad and unqualified," and
       obviously applies outside of antitrust and similar laws).

[50]   Id. See also Norfolk & Western Ry. v. Train Dispatchers, 499 U.S. 117, 129
       (1991) ("the canon does not control . . . when the whole context dictates a
       different conclusion"); United States v. Turkette, 452 U.S. 576, 580-82
       (1981) (appeals court erred in finding that a second category was merely a
       more general description of the first; context and language instead reveal
       two contrasting categories).

[51]   REED DICKERSON, THE INTERPRETATION AND APPLICATION OF
       STATUTES, 234 (1975).

[52]   Hammock v. Loan and Trust Co., 105 U.S. (15 Otto) 77, 84-85 (1881)
       (disregarding a comma). See also United States v. Shreveport Grain &
       Elevator Co., 287 U.S. 77, 82-83 (1932) (also disregarding a comma).

[53]   See, e.g., Arcadia v. Ohio Power Co., 498 U.S. 73, 78 (1990) ("In casual
       conversation, perhaps, such absent-minded duplication and omission are
       possible, but Congress is not presumed to draft its laws that way.").

[54]   Ingalls Shipbuilding v. Director, OWCP, 519 U.S. 248, 255 (1997) (present
       tense of verb is an element of plain meaning); Dole Food Co. v. Patrickson,
       538 U.S. 468, 478 (2003) (interpretation required by "plain text" derived
       from present tense).

[55]   55 United States Nat'l Bank of Oregon v. Independent Ins. Agents, 508 U.S.
       439, 454 (1993).

[56]   Id. See also Costanzo v. Tillinghast, 287 U.S. 341, 344 (1932) ("It has often
       been said that punctuation is not decisive of the construction of a statute. . . .
       Upon like principle we should not apply the rules of syntax to defeat the
       evident legislative intent.").

[57]   Independent Ins. Agents, supra n.55, 508 U.S. at 462. This "unusual case"
       held that Congress did not in 1918 repeal a statutory provision enacted in

1916 allowing national banks located in small communities to sell insurance. The "scrivener's error" had erroneously credited the 1916 enactment with having amended a provision that was repealed by the 1918 enactment.

[58] United States v. Ron Pair Enterprises, 489 U.S. 235, 241 (1989).

[59] Nobelman v. American Savings Bank, 508 U.S. 324, 330-3 1 (1993). See also Lamie v. United States Trustee, 540 U.S. 526, 534 (2004) ("The statute is awkward, and even ungrammatical; but that does not make it ambiguous").

[60] United States v. X-Citement Video, Inc., 513 U.S. 64, 68 (1994). Justice Scalia, dissenting, insisted that the language was perfectly clear, and that the rejected interpretation was "the only grammatical reading." Id. at 81.

[61] Montclair v. Ramsdell, 107 U.S. 147, 152 (1883).

[62] Astoria Federal Savings & Loan Ass'n v. Solimino, 501 U.S. 104, 112 (1991); Sprietsma v. Mercury Marine, 537 U.S. 51, 63 (2003) (interpreting word "law" broadly could render word "regulation" superfluous in preemption clause applicable to a state "law or regulation"). See also Bailey v. United States, 516 U.S. 137, 146 (1995) ("we assume that Congress used two terms because it intended each term to have a particular, nonsuperfluous meaning") (rejecting interpretation that would have made "uses" and "carries" redundant in statute penalizing using or carrying a firearm in commission of offense). The presumption also guides interpretation of "redundancies across statutes." Two overlapping statutes may be given effect so long as there is no "positive repugnance" between them. Connecticut Nat'l Bank v. Germain, 503 U.S. 249, 253 (1992) (finding that, in spite of considerable overlap between two provisions, each addressed matters that the other did not).

[63] United States v. Wilson, 503 U.S. 333, 336 (1992) (nonetheless attributing no significance to deletion of a reference to the Attorney General; the reference "was simply lost in the shuffle" of a comprehensive statutory revision that had various unrelated purposes); Stone v. INS, 514 U.S. 386, 397 (1995) ("When Congress acts to amend a statute, we presume it intends its amendment to have real and substantial effect."). There is an exception for minor, unexplained changes in phraseology made during recodification — changes that courts generally assume are "not intended to alter the statute's scope." Walters v. National Ass'n of Radiation Survivors, 473 U.S. 305, 318 (1985).

[64] Ratzlaf v. United States, 510 U.S. 135, 140-41 (1994).

[65] See, e.g., Moskal v. United States, 498 U.S. 103 (1990). Dissenting Justice
      Scalia objected to the Court's straining to avoid holding that "falsely made"
      is redundant in the federal forgery statute, which prohibits receipt of
      "falsely made, forged, altered, or counterfeited securities." "The principle
      [against mere surplusage] is sound, but its limitation ('if possible') should
      be observed. It should not be used to distort ordinary meaning. Nor should it
      be applied to obvious instances of iteration to which lawyers, alas, are
      particularly addicted . . . ." Id. at 120.

[66] Iselin v. United States, 270 U.S. 245, 250 (1926). See also Lamie v. United
      States Trustee, 540 U.S. 526, 537 (2004) (courts should not add an "absent
      word" to a statute; "there is a basic difference between filling a gap left by
      Congress' silence and rewriting rules that Congress has affirmatively and
      specifically enacted"). Obviously, the line between the permissible filling in
      of statutory gaps and the impermissible adding of statutory content may be
      indistinct in some instances, and statutory context, congressional purpose,
      and overriding presumptions may tip the scales. For example, the Court
      made no mention of the "absent word" rule in holding that a reference to
      "any entity" actually meant "any private entity" in the context of
      preemption. Nixon v. Missouri Municipal League, 541 U.S. 125 (2004)
      (preemption of state laws that prohibit "any entity" from providing
      telecommunications service does not preempt a state law prohibiting local
      governments from providing such service).

[67] Ratzlaf v. United States, 510 U.S. 135, 143 (1994). See also Gustafson v.
      Alloyd Co., 513 U.S. 561, 570 (1995); and Wisconsin Dep't of Revenue v.
      William Wrigley, Jr. Co., 505 U.S. 214, 225 (1992). The Court cited this
      passage of Wrigley to invoke a quite different principle, described as "the
      established canon" that "similar [rather than identical] language" in the
      same section of a statute "must be accorded a consistent [rather than the
      same] meaning." National Credit Union Admin. v. First Nat'l Bank & Trust
      Co., 522 U.S. 479, 501(1998).

[68] Brown v. Gardner, 513 U.S. 115, 118 (1994); Reno v. Bossier Parish Sch.
      Bd., 528 U.S. 320, 329-30 (2000).

[69] Atlantic Cleaners & Dyers, Inc. v. United States, 286 U.S. 427, 433 (1933).
      See also Robinson v. Shell Oil Co., 519 U.S. 337, 342-43 (1997) (term
      "employees" means current employees only in some sections of Title VII of
      Civil Rights Act, but in other sections includes former employees); United
      States v. Cleveland Indians Baseball Co., 532 U.S. 200 (2001) (different
      statutory contexts of worker eligibility for Social Security benefits and
      "administrability" of tax rules justify different interpretations); General

Dynamics Land Systems, Inc. v. Cline, 540 U.S. 581, 594-595 (2004) (word "age" means "old age" when included in the term "age discrimination" in the Age Discrimination in Employment Act even though it is used in its primary sense elsewhere in the act). For disagreement about the appropriateness of applying this limitation, contrast the Court's opinion in Gustafson v. Alloyd Co., supra n.67, 513 U.S. at 573, with the dissenting opinion of Justice Thomas in the same case, id. at 590 (interpreting a definition that, by its terms, was applicable "unless the context otherwise requires").

[70] Keene Corp. v. United States, 508 U.S. 200, 208 (1993) (quoting Russello v. United States, 464 U.S. 16, 23 (1983)). See also Bailey v. United States. 516 U.S. 137, 146 (1995) (distinction in one provision between "used" and "intended to be used" creates implication that related provision's reliance on "use" alone refers to actual and not intended use); and Bates v. United States, 522 U.S. 23, 29 (1997) (inclusion of "intent to defraud" language in one provision and exclusion in a parallel provision).

[71] Lindh v. Murphy, 521 U.S. 320, 330 (1997) (statute was explicit in making one section applicable to habeas cases pending on date of enactment, but was silent as to parallel provision).

[72] King v. St. Vincent's Hospital, 502 U.S. 215, 220-21 (1991) ("given the examples of affirmative limitations on reemployment benefits conferred by neighboring provisions, we infer that the simplicity of subsection (d) was deliberate, consistent with a plain meaning to provide its benefit without conditions on length of service").

[73] Chapman v. United States, 500 U.S. 453, 459 (1991) (fact that, with respect to some drugs, Congress distinguished between a "mixture or substance" containing the drug and a "pure" drug refutes the argument that Congress' failure to so distinguish with respect to LSD was inadvertent).

[74] See Field v. Mans, 516 U.S. 59, 67 (1995) ("without more, the ['negative pregnant'] inference might be a helpful one," but other interpretive guides prove more useful).

[75] Central Bank of Denver v. First Interstate Bank, 511 U.S. 164, 176-77 (1994). See also Franklin Nat'l Bank v. New York, 347 U.S. 373, 378 (1954) (finding "no indication that Congress intended to make this phase of national banking subject to local restrictions, as it has done by express language in several other instances"); Meghrig v. KFC Western, Inc., 516 U.S. 479, 485 (1996) ("Congress . . . demonstrated in CERCLA that it knew how to provide for the recovery of cleanup costs, and . . . the language used to define the remedies under RCRA does not provide that remedy"); FCC v.

NextWave Personal Communications, Inc., 537 U.S. 293, 302 (2003) (when Congress has intended to create exceptions to bankruptcy law requirements, "it has done so clearly and expressly"); Dole Food Co. v. Patrickson, 538 U.S. 468, 476 (2003) (Congress knows how to refer to an "owner" "in other than the formal sense," and did not do so in the Foreign Sovereign Immunities Act's definition of foreign state "instrumentality"); Whitfield v. United States, 543 U.S. 209, 216 (2005) (Congress has imposed an explicit overt act requirement in 22 conspiracy statutes, yet has not done so in the provision governing conspiracy to commit money laundering).

[76] See, e.g., Jackson v. Birmingham Bd. of Educ., 544 U.S. 167 (2005) (Title IX's prohibition on sex discrimination encompasses retaliation despite absence of an explicit prohibition on retaliation such as those contained in Title VII, the ADA, and the Age Discrimination in Employment Act).

[77] See, e.g., the provisions of the Plant Variety Protection Act at issue in Asgrow Seed Co. v. Winterboer, 513 U.S. 179 (1995). Justice Scalia in his opinion for the Court in Asgrow called 7 U.S.C. § 2543 a "verbal maze," and conceded that "it is quite impossible to make complete sense of the provision." Id. at 185-86. In another case, the Court found statutory language "incoherent" due to use of three different and conflicting standards identifying an evidentiary burden. Concrete Pipe & Products v. Construction Laborers Pension Trust, 508 U.S. 602, 627 (1993). The Court resolved the issue by treating the "incoherence" as ambiguity, and by applying the one possible construction that did not raise constitutional issues. Id. at 628-30.

[78] See, e.g., Landgraf v. USI Film Products, 511 U.S. 244, 263 (1994) ("the history of the 1991 [Civil Rights] Act conveys the impression that the legislators agreed to disagree about whether and to what extent the Act would apply to preenactment conduct").

[79] FMC Corp. v. Holliday, 498 U.S. 52, 66 (1990) (Justice Stevens, dissenting, objecting to Court's interpretation of convoluted preemption language in ERISA).

[80] 80 Burns v. United States, 501 U.S. 129, 136 (1991) (quoting Illinois Dep't of Public Aid v. Schweiker, 707 F.2d 273, 277 (7th Cir. 1983)).

[81] Director, OWCP v. Newport News Shipbuilding Co., 514 U.S. 122 (1995) (agency in its governmental capacity is not a "person adversely affected or aggrieved" for purposes of judicial review). See also United States v. Bestfoods, 524 U.S. 51, 62 (1998) ("against this venerable common-law backdrop, the congressional silence is audible"); Elkins v. Moreno, 435 U.S. 647, 666 (1978) (absence of reference to an immigrant's intent to remain

citizen of foreign country is "pregnant" when contrasted with other provisions of "comprehensive and complete" immigration code); Meyer v. Holley, 537 U.S. 280 (2003) (ordinary rules of vicarious liability apply to tort actions under the Fair Housing Act; statutory silence as to vicarious liability contrasts with explicit departures in other laws).

[82]   Whitman v. American Trucking Ass'ns, Inc., 531 U.S. 457, 468 (2001). See also MCI Telecommunications Corp. v. AT&T, 512 U.S. 218, 231 (1994) (conferral of authority to "modify" rates was not a cryptic conferral of authority to make filing of rates voluntary); Director of Revenue of Mo. v. CoBank, ACB, 531 U.S. 316, 323 (2001) ("it would be surprising, indeed," if Congress had effected a "radical" change in the law "sub silentio" via "technical and conforming amendments").

[83]   FDA v. Brown & Williamson Tobacco Corp., 529 U.S. 120, 160 (2000). Ordinarily the Court does not require reference to specific applications of general authority, but in this instance ("hardly an ordinary case") the Court majority attached importance to the FDA's longstanding disavowal of regulatory authority, and to subsequently enacted tobacco- specific legislation that stopped short of conferring authority to ban sale of the product.

[84]   Andrus v. Glover Const. Co., 446 U.S. 608, 616-17 (1980) (citing Continental Casualty Co. v. United States, 314 U.S. 527, 533 (1942)).

[85]   Demarest v. Manspeaker, 498 U.S. 184, 188 (1991). Congress quickly acted to override this result and prohibit payment of witness fees to prisoners, P.L. 102-4 17, 106 Stat. 2138 (1992), the House Judiciary Committee expressing the belief that "Congress never intended" that prisoners be paid witness fees. H.Rept. 102-194, 102d Cong., 1st Sess. 2 (1991).

[86]   NationsBank v. Variable Annuity Life Ins. Co., 513 U.S. 251, 257 (1995) (endorsing Comptroller of the Currency's interpretation).

[87]   Wisconsin Dep't of Revenue v. William Wrigley, Jr. Co., 505 U.S. 214, 23 1-32 (1992) (company's activities within the state clearly exceeded de minimis, so company was subject to state franchise tax). See also Abbott Laboratories v. Portland Retail Druggists, 425 U.S. 1, 18 (1976) (occasional emergency dispensation of drugs to walk-in patients is de minimis deviation from Robinson-Patman Act's exemption for hospitals' purchase of supplies "for their own use"); Industrial Ass'n v. United States, 268 U.S. 64, 68 (1925) (3 or 4 "sporadic and doubtful instances" of interference with interstate commerce in what was in essence an intrastate matter were insufficient to establish a violation of the Sherman Act).

[88] Astoria Federal Savings & Loan Ass'n v. Solimino, 501 U.S. 104, 108-09 (1991).

[89] Judge Wald described one such presumption as requiring that Congress "signal[ ] its intention in neon lights." Patricia M. Wald, *Some Observations on the Use of Legislative History in the 1981 Supreme Court Term*, 68 IOWA L. REV. 195, 208 (1983). See generally pp. 206-14 of the article. See also William N. Eskridge, Jr. and Philip P. Frickey, *Quasi-Constitutional Law: Clear Statement Rules as Constitutional Lawmaking*, 45 VAND. L. REV. 593 (1992).

[90] Midlantic Nat'l Bank v. New Jersey Dep't of Envt'l Protection, 474 U.S. 494, 501 (1986)(quoting Edmonds v. Compagnie Generale Transatlantique, 443 U.S. 256, 266-67 (1979)).

[91] Pennsylvania Pub. Welfare Dep't v. Davenport, 495 U.S. 552, 563 (1990) (nonetheless finding that the statutory language plainly evidenced an intent to depart from past practice).

[92] Rice v. Santa Fe Elevator Corp., 331 U.S. 218, 230 (1947); Wisconsin Public Intervenor v. Mortier, 501 U.S. 597, 605 (1991).

[93] A statement asserting preemption or disclaiming intent to preempt must be clear not only as to preemptive intent, but also as to scope. In International Paper Co. v. Ouellette, 479 U.S. 481 (1987), for example, the Court ruled that some aspects of state law were preempted in spite of a savings clause in the citizens suit provision of the Clean Water Act declaring that "nothing in this section" should be read as affecting an injured party's right to seek relief under any statute or common law. Other parts of the act outside of the citizens suit section were read as implying preemption. "Because we do not believe Congress intended to undermine this carefully drawn statute [leaving a source state responsible for control of point-source discharges within its boundaries] through a general savings clause, we conclude that the CWA precludes a court from applying the law of an affected state against an out-of-state source." Id. at 484.

[94] Gregory v. Ashcroft, 501 U.S. 452 (1991).

[95] Id. at 461. See also Nixon v. Missouri Municipal League, 541 U.S. 1 25 (2004) (indicating that the plain statement rule is also appropriate for laws "interposing federal authority between a State and its municipal subdivisions").

[96] Hoffman v. Connecticut Income Maint. Dep't, 492 U.S. 96, 101 (1989) (quoting Atascadero State Hosp. v. Scanlon, 473 U.S. 234, 242 (1985)).

[97] 517 U.S. 44, 73 (1996).

[98] See, e.g., the Assimilative Crimes Statute, 18 U.S.C. § 13, governing crimes within the special maritime and territorial jurisdiction of the United States.

[99] Jerome v. United States, 318 U.S. 101, 104 (1943). Arguably, the Jerome Court actually overstated the case, citing United States v. Pelzer, 312 U.S. 399, 402 (1941), for the proposition that "the application of federal legislation is nationwide." Pelzer was far less sweeping, holding only that "in light of their general purpose to establish a nationwide scheme of taxation uniform in its application," provisions of the revenue laws "should not be taken as subject to state control or limitation unless the language or necessary implication of the section involved makes its application dependent on state law." 312 U.S. at 402-03.

[100] Dickerson v. New Banner Inst., 460 U.S. 103, 119 (1983) (quoting NLRB v. Randolph Elec. Membership Corp., 343 F.2d 60, 62-63 (4th Cir. 1965)).

[101] 101 United States v. Nordic Village, Inc., 503 U.S. 30, 34 (1992); Ardestani v. INS, 502 U.S. 129, 137 (1991) (partial waiver).

[102] United States v. Nordic Village, supra n.101, 503 U.S. at 37. For criticism of the rule, see John Copeland Nagle, Waiving Sovereign Immunity in an Age of Clear Statement Rules, 1995 WISC. L. REV. 771, 836.

[103] UMW v. United States, 330 U.S. 258, 272 (1947) (United States is not an "employer" for purposes of the Norris-LaGuardia Act); Vermont Agency of Nat. Resources v. United States ex rel. Stevens, 529 U.S. 765, 780-8 1 (2000) (state is not a "person" for purposes of qui tam liability under the False Claims Act).

[104] Gozlon-Peretz v. United States, 498 U.S. 395, 404 (1991). Ordinarily, and in the absence of special circumstances, the law does not recognize fractions of the day, so a law becomes effective "from the first moment" of the effective date. Lapeyre v. United States, 17 Wall. 191, 198 (1872). However, "whenever it becomes important to the ends of justice . . . the law will look into fractions of a day." Louisville v. Savings Bank, 104 U.S. 469, 474 (1881). See Burgess v. Salmon, 97 U.S. 381 (1878) (a law signed in the afternoon could not be applied to fine a person for actions he had completed on the morning of the same day); United States v. Will, 449 U.S. 200, 225 n.29 (1980) (a judicial salary increase had taken effect at the beginning of the day, and was already in effect when the President later in the day signed legislation reducing cost-of-living increases).

[105] Landgraf v. USI Film Products, 511 U.S. 244, 272-73 (1994) (finding no such clearly expressed congressional intent with respect to the civil rights law's new compensatory and punitive damages remedies and the associated right to a jury trial).

[106] Art. I, § 9, cl. 3 prohibits Congress from enacting ex post facto laws; Art. I, § 10 applies the prohibition to the states. See Lynce v. Mathis, 519 U.S. 433, 439 (1997); and Johnson v. United States, 529 U.S. 694, 701 (2000), for general discussion.

[107] United States v. Jin Fuey Moy, 241 U.S. 394, 401 (1916); Almendarez-Torres v. United States, 523 U.S. 224, 237-38 (1998); Jones v. United States, 529 U.S. 848, 857 (2000). See also Ashwander v. Tennessee Valley Authority, 297 U.S. 288, 347 (1936) (J. Brandeis, concurring) ("The Court will not pass upon a constitutional question, although properly presented by the record, if there is also present some other ground upon which the case may be disposed of. [...] Thus, if a case can be decided upon two grounds, one involving a constitutional question, the other a question of statutory construction or general law, the Court will decide only the latter.").

[108] DeBartolo Corp. v. Florida Gulf Coast Trades Council, 485 U.S. 568, 575 (1988) (quoting Hooper v. California, 155 U.S. 648, 657 (1895)). Accord, Burns v. United States, 501 U.S. 129, 138 (1991); Gollust v. Mendell, 501 U.S. 115, 126 (1991).

[109] Almendarez-Torres v. United States, 523 U.S. 224, 239 (1998) (citing Rust v. Sullivan, 500 U.S. 173, 191 (1991), in which the Court concluded, over the dissent of four Justices, that abortion counseling regulations "do not raise the sort of 'grave and doubtful constitutional questions,'. . . that would lead us to assume Congress did not intend to authorize their issuance").

[110] EEOC v. Arabian American Oil Co., 499 U.S. 244, 248 (1991) (quoting Foley Bros, Inc. v. Filardo, 336 U.S. 281, 285 (1949)). See also Smith v. United States, 507 U.S. 197, 203- 04 (1993) (interpretation of Federal Tort Claims Act as inapplicable in Antarctica is reinforced by presumption against extraterritorial application). Cf. Hartford Fire Ins. Co. v. California, 509 U.S. 764, 796 (1993) (Sherman Act applies to foreign conduct producing, and intended to produce, substantial effects in United States).

[111] Bowen v. Michigan Academy of Family Physicians, 476 U.S. 667, 670 (1986). See also McNary v. Haitian Refugee Center, 498 U.S. 479, 496 (1991) ("it is most unlikely that Congress intended to foreclose all forms of meaningful judicial review," given the presumption "that Congress legislates with knowledge of our basic rules of statutory construction").

[112] 5 U.S.C. § 704.

[113] 5 U.S.C. § 701(a).

[114] Lindahl v. OPM, 470 U.S. 768, 778 (1985) (provision in Civil Service Retirement Act stating that OPM's "decisions . . . concerning these matters are final and conclusive and are not subject to review" interpreted as

precluding review only of OPM's factual determinations, but as not precluding review of legal interpretations). The Lindahl Court contrasted other statutory language said to be "far more unambiguous and comprehensive" in precluding review. Id. at 779-80 & n.13 (citing 5 U.S.C. § 8128(b) ("action of the Secretary . . . is final and conclusive for all purposes and with respect to all questions of law and fact"); and 38 U.S.C. § 211(a) ("decisions of the Administrator on any question of law or fact . . . shall be final and conclusive and no other official or any court of the United States shall have power or jurisdiction to review any such decision").

[115] Abbott Labs. v. Gardner, 387 U.S. 136, 140 (1967) (pre-enforcement review of regulations under Federal Food, Drug, and Cosmetic Act is not precluded as a result of negative inference arising from fact that act has explicit authorization for review of other kinds of regulations).

[116] Block v. Community Nutrition Inst., 467 U.S. 340, 349 (1984) (judicial review of milk marketing orders not available to consumers). Accord, United States v. Fausto, 484 U.S. 439, 452 (1988) (congressional intent to preclude judicial review is clear from the purposes of the Civil Service Reform Act, from the entirety of its text, and from the structure of the statutory scheme).

[117] Chevron U.S.A. v. Natural Resources Defense Council, 467 U.S. 837 (1984).

[118] Christensen v. Harris County, 529 U.S. 576 (2000).

[119] United States v. Mead Corp., 533 U.S. 218 (2001).

[120] Mead Corp., 533 U.S. at 229.

[121] 323 U.S. 134 (1944).

[122] Chevron, 467 U.S. at 842.

[123] 467 U.S. at 843 n.9.

[124] Id. at 843.

[125] See, e.g., Sullivan v. Everhart, 494 U.S. 83 (1990) (regulations are a reasonable interpretation of Social Security Act); Smiley v. Citibank (South Dakota), 517 U.S. 735 (1996) (upholding Comptroller of the Currency's interpretation of 1864 Bank Act); and Lopez v. Davis, 531 U.S. 230, 240 (2001) (Bureau of Prisons regulation denying early release is reasonable interpretation of discretionary authority).

[126] See, e.g., Sullivan v. Zebley, 493 U.S. 521 (1990) (regulations "are simply inconsistent with the statutory standard"); and Dole v. Steelworkers, 494 U.S. 26 (1990) (deference to OMB interpretation of Paperwork Reduction Act is foreclosed by Court's finding of clear congressional intent to contrary).

[127] Whitman v. American Trucking Ass'ns, Inc., 531 U.S. 457 (2001).

[128] See, e.g., Dunn v. CFTC, 519 U.S. 465, 473-74 (1997) (legislative history supports Court's conclusion that statute is clear and agency's interpretation is untenable). See also Babbitt v. Sweet Home Chapter, 515 U.S. 687, 708 (1995) (Court concludes, "based on the text, structure, and legislative history of the ESA, that the Secretary reasonably construed the intent of Congress" in defining "harm").

[129] See, e.g., K Mart Corp. v. Cartier, Inc., 486 U.S. 281, 291 (1988) (courts should look "to the particular statutory language at issue, as well as the language and design of the statute as a whole" in order to ascertain statute's "plain meaning"); Ohio Pub. Employees Retirement System v. Betts, 492 U.S. 158, 171 (1989) ("no deference is due to agency interpretations at odds with the plain language of the statute itself").

[130] See, e.g., MCI Telecommunications Corp. v. AT&T Co., 512 U.S. 218, 231 (1994) ("it is highly unlikely that Congress would leave the determination of whether an industry will be entirely, or even substantially, rate-regulated to agency discretion").

[131] FDA v. Brown & Williamson Tobacco Corp., 529 U.S. 120, 160 (2000).

[132] The subsequent legislation created "a distinct regulatory scheme for tobacco products."529 U.S. at 159. As Justice Breyer's dissent pointed out, tobacco products clearly fell within the generally worded jurisdictional definitions of the Food, Drug, and Cosmetic Act, and it was also clear that Congress had not spoken directly to the issue anywhere else in that act. 529 U.S. at 162. The Court's different resolution of a similar issue concerning patent protection for plant breeding illustrates that a subsequently enacted "distinct regulatory scheme" does not always trump general authority. The Court ruled in 1980 and again in 2001 that neither the Plant Patent Act of 1930 nor the Plant Variety Protection Act — both premised on the understanding that the Patent and Trademark Office lacked authority to issue plant patents under its general utility patent authority — deprived the Office of authority to issue plant patents pursuant to that general authority. Diamond v. Chakrabarty, 447 U.S. 3 18 (1980); J.E.M. Ag Supply, Inc. v. Farm Advantage, Inc., 534 U.S. 124 (2001).

[133] Solid Waste Agency v. Army Corps of Engineers, 531 U.S. 159, 172 (2001).

[134] Smiley v. Citibank (South Dakota), 517 U.S. 735, 740 (1996) (upholding regulation issued more than 100 years after statute's enactment).

[135] Id. at 742. In other words, the Court presumes "that Congress, when it left ambiguity in a statute meant for implementation by an agency, understood

that the ambiguity would be resolved, first and foremost, by the agency . . . ." Id. at 740-41.

[136] 545 U.S. 967 (2005).

[137] Id. at 982.

[138] Christensen v. Harris County, 529 U.S. 576, 587 (2000).

[139] Skidmore v. Swift & Co., 323 U.S. 134 (1944).

[140] Christensen v. Harris County, 529 U.S. at 587. As the Court put it in Skidmore, agency interpretations "constitute a body of experience and informed judgment to which courts and litigants may properly resort . . . . The weight of such a judgment in a particular case will depend upon the thoroughness evident in its consideration, the validity of its reasoning, its consistency with earlier and later pronouncements, and all those factors which give it power to persuade, if lacking power to control." 323 U.S. at 140.

[141] See, e.g., Aluminum Co. v. Central Lincoln Util. Dist., 467 U.S. 380, 390 (1984).

[142] See, e.g., Investment Co. Inst. v. Camp, 401 U.S. 617, 626-27 (1971).

[143] See, e.g., Udall v. Tallman, 380 U.S. 1, 16 (1965).

[144] See, e.g., General Electric Co. v. Gilbert, 429 U.S. 125, 142-43 (1976).

[145] United States v. Fausto, 484 U.S. 439, 453 (1988).

[146] Watt v. Alaska, 451 U.S. 259, 267 (1981). See also Lewis v. Lewis & Clark Marine, Inc., 531 U.S. 438 (2001) (reconciling "tension" between the saving to suitors clause and the Limitation of Liability Act); Ruckelshaus v. Monsanto Co., 467 U.S. 986, 10 17-18 (1984) (rejecting a contention that the Federal Insecticide, Fungicide, and Rodenticide Act repealed by implication a Tucker Act remedy for governmental taking of property without just compensation, and reconciling the two statutes by implying a requirement that remedies under FIFRA must be exhausted before relief under the Tucker Act could be obtained). But see Stewart v. Smith, 673 F.2d 485, 492 (D.C. Cir. 1982) (interpreting a statute authorizing agency heads to set maximum age limits for law enforcement officers as an exception to the Age Discrimination in Employment Act). Even though the laws might have been harmonized through a "strained reading," the court concluded that doing so would thwart the maximum age law's sense and purpose. The Stewart court relied on legislative history to find a "clear" congressional intent "to employ maximum entry ages as a means towards securing a 'young and vigorous' work force of law enforcement officers," and concluded that furtherance of this policy required "consideration of factors not ordinarily accounted for" under ADEA procedures.

[147] Watt v. Alaska, supra n.146, at 266.

[148] Posadas v. National City Bank, 296 U.S. 497, 503 (1936).

[149] Rodriguez v. United States, 480 U.S. 522, 524 (1987) (citations omitted). See also Morton v. Mancari, 417 U.S. 535, 550-51 (1974).

[150] For an instance in which the Court arguably found repeal by implication, see Argentine Republic v. Amerada Hess Shipping Corp., 488 U.S. 428, 438 (1989) (concluding that Congress had intended to "deal comprehensively with the subject of foreign sovereign immunity in the [Foreign Sovereign Immunities Act of 1976]," and that consequently suit against the Argentine Republic could not be brought under the Alien Tort Statute). But see Branch v. Smith, 538 U.S. 254, 293 (2003), in which Justice O'Connor asserted that the Court last found a repeal by implication in 1975, in Gordon v. New York Stock Exchange, 422 U.S. 659 (antitrust laws impliedly repealed (in part) by Securities Exchange Act).

[151] Friedrich v. City of Chicago, 888 F.2d 511, 516 (7th Cir. 1989). Judge Posner describes the assumption on which the canon rests — that Congress surveys and envisions the whole body of law before legislating — as "unrealistic": how could Congress do so, he has questioned, "given the vast expanse of legislation that has never been repealed and the even vaster expanse of judicial and administrative rulings glossing that legislation." In re Doctors' Hospital of Hyde Park, 337 F.3d 951, 960 (7th Cir. 2003). On the plus side, the rule serves the "superior values of harmonizing different statutes and constraining judicial discretion in the interpretation of the laws." Astoria Federal Savings & Loan Ass'n v. Solimino, 501 U.S. 104, 109 (1991).

[152] Pullen v. Morgenthau, 73 F.2d 281 (2d Cir. 1934).

[153] SUTHERLAND, STATUTES AND STATUTORY CONSTRUCTION § 23:18 (Norman J. Singer ed., 6th ed. 2002 rev.).

[154] Id.

[155] TVA v. Hill, 437 U.S. 153, 190 (1978) (emphasis added).

[156] United States v. Will, 449 U.S. 200, 222 (1980).

[157] United States v. Gradwell, 243 U.S. 476, 485 (1917).

[158] Hughey v. United States, 495 U.S. 411, 422 (1990). See also United States v. Granderson, 511 U.S. 39, 54 (1994) ("In these circumstances — where text, structure, and [legislative] history fail to establish that the Government's position is unambiguously correct — we apply the rule of lenity and resolve the ambiguity in [the defendant's] favor"); Cleveland v. United States, 531 U.S. 12, 25 (2000) (before choosing a "harsher alternative" interpretation of the mail fraud statute, "it is appropriate . . . to

require that Congress should have spoken in language that is clear and definite").

[159] Ratzlaf v. United States, 510 U.S. 135, 148-49 (1994) (quoting Boyle v. United States, 283 U.S. 25, 27 (1931) (Justice Holmes for Court)).

[160] 160 Beecham v. United States, 511 U.S. 368, 374 (1994) (quoting Chapman v. United States, 500 U.S. 453, 463-64 (1991)). Accord, National Org. for Women v. Scheidler, 510 U.S. 249, 262 (1994).

[161] United States v. X-Citement Video, Inc., 513 U.S. 64, 72 (1994).

[162] "Our reluctance to simply follow the most grammatical reading of the statute is heightened by our cases interpreting criminal statutes to include broadly applicable scienter requirements, even where the statute by its terms does not contain them." X-Citement Video, 513 U.S. at 70. See also Staples v. United States, 511 U.S. 600 (1994) (National Firearms Act interpreted to require that defendant knew that the weapon he possessed was a "firearm" subject to the act's registration requirements); and Liparota v. United States, 471 U.S. 419 (1985) ("knowingly" read as modifying not only operative verbs "uses . . . or possesses," but also "in a manner not authorized").

[163] Posters <N' Things, Ltd. v. United States, 511 U.S. 513 (1994) (interpreting drug paraphernalia law as requiring that merchant knew that customers in general are likely to use the merchandise with drugs).

[164] See, e.g., United States v. Dotterweich, 320 U.S. 277 (1943) (upholding punishment of corporate officer whose company shipped misbranded and adulterated drugs in violation of Food and Drug laws); United States v. Freed, 401 U.S. 601 (1971) (upholding conviction under National Firearms Act for possession of unregistered hand grenades; Act does not and need not require proof of knowledge that weapons were not registered).

[165] Compare United States v. Freed, 401 U.S. 601 (1971) (knowledge of unregistered status of hand grenades not required for conviction under National Firearms Act) with Staples v. United States, 511 U.S. 600 (1994) (conviction under the Firearms Act must be predicated on defendant's knowledge of the particular characteristics making a semi-automatic rifle convertible to a machine gun and hence subject to registration requirement). The Staples Court distinguished Freed, partly on the basis that, given the "long tradition of widespread lawful gun ownership by private individuals in this country," possession of a semi-automatic rifle should not be equated with possession of hand grenades. See 511 U.S. at 610-12.

[166] United States v. United States Gypsum Co., 438 U.S. 422, 438 (1978) (applying principle to Sherman Act violation).

[167] For not-so-recent reliance on the canon, see Peyton v. Rowe, 391 U.S. 54, 65 (1968) (petitioner is "in custody" in violation of Constitution for purposes of federal habeas corpus statute if any of consecutive sentences he is scheduled to serve was imposed as a result of deprivation of his rights); Tcherepnin v. Knight, 389 U.S. 332, 336 (1967) (term "security" should be construed broadly, in part because "Securities Exchange Act quite clearly falls into the category of remedial legislation"); and Chisholm v. Georgia, 2 U.S. (2 Dall.) 419, 475 (1793) (opinion of Chief Justice Jay) (Constitution's extension of judicial power over controversies between a state and citizens of another state is "remedial, [and] therefore, to be construed liberally").

[168] The Court once referred to a variant of the canon (a statute should be liberally construed to achieve its purposes) as "that last redoubt of losing causes," explaining that "[e]very statute proposes, not only to achieve certain ends, but also to achieve them by particular means — and there is often a considerable legislative battle over what those means ought to be." Director, OWCP v. Newport News Shipbuilding, 514 U.S. 122, 135-36 (1995).

[169] Justice Scalia has inveighed against the maxim in a lecture reprinted as a law review article, calling it a "prime example[ ] of lego-babble." The rule, Justice Scalia concluded, "is both of indeterminate coverage (since no one knows what a 'remedial statute' is) and of indeterminate effect (since no one knows how liberal is a liberal construction)." Antonin Scalia, Assorted Canards of Legal Analysis, 40 CASE W. RES. L. REV. 581, 586 (1989-90).

[170] See, e.g., Smith v. Heckler, 820 F.2d 1093, 1095 (9th Cir. 1987) (Social Security Act "is remedial, to be construed liberally . . . and not so as to withhold benefits in marginal cases").

[171] This is not to say, however, that the same fairness considerations that underlie the rule of lenity justify application of the "remedial statute" rule.

[172] 172 See, e.g., King v. St. Vincent's Hosp., 502 U.S. 215, 220 n.9 (1991) ("provisions for benefits to members of the Armed Services are to be construed in the beneficiaries' favor"); FDIC v. Meyer, 510 U.S. 471, 480 (1994) ("sue-and-be-sued" waivers of sovereign immunity should be liberally construed).

[173] 173 See, e.g., Felder v. Casey, 487 U.S. 131, 149 (1988) ("the Congress which enacted [42 U.S.C.] § 1983 over 100 years ago would have rejected [a requirement of exhaustion of state remedies] as inconsistent with the remedial purposes of its broad statute"); Sullivan v. Little Hunting Park, 396 U.S. 229, 237 (1969) ("A narrow construction of § 1982 would be inconsistent with the broad and sweeping nature of the protection meant to

be afforded by § 1 of the Civil Rights Act of 1866"); Northeast Marine Terminal v. Caputo, 432 U.S. 249, 268 (1977) ("The language of the 1972 Amendments [to the LHWCA] is broad and suggests that we should take an expansive view of the extended coverage. Indeed such a construction is appropriate for this remedial legislation.").

[174] Bryan v. Itasca County, 426 U.S. 373, 392 (1976) (quoting Alaska Pacific Fisheries v.United States, 248 U.S. 78, 89 (1918)). An even less restrictive statement is the following: "statutes are to be construed liberally in favor of the Indians, with ambiguous provisions interpreted to their benefit." Montana v. Blackfeet Tribe, 471 U.S. 759, 766 (1985).

[175] See, e.g., Washington v. Confederated Tribes, 447 U.S. 134, 154 (1980) (tribal sovereignty is subordinate only to the federal government, not to the states); Bryan v. Itasca County, 426 U.S. 373, 393 (1976) (states may tax reservation Indians only if Congress has indicated its consent); Hagen v. Utah, 510 U.S. 399, 411-12 (1994) (mild presumption against statutory diminishment of reservation land).

[176] See, e.g., California v. Cabazon Band of Mission Indians, 480 U.S. 202, 2 14-22 (1987) (federal policy promoting tribal self-government and self-sufficiency, reflected in numerous statutes, is frustrated by state and county restrictions on operation of bingo and card games, profits from which were Tribes' sole source of income).

[177] See, e.g., Negonsott v. Samuels, 507 U.S. 99, 110 (1993) (fact that Kansas Act unambiguously confers jurisdiction on Kansas courts over crimes on reservations makes resort to canon inappropriate).

[178] Pennhurst State Sch. & Hosp. v. Halderman, 451 U.S. 1, 19 n. 14 (1981) (quoting United States v. Oregon & California R.R., 164 U.S. 526, 541 (1896) and Cornell v. Coyne, 192 U.S. 418, 430 (1904), and citing United States v. Fisher, 2 Cranch 358, 386 (1805) and Yazoo & Mississippi Valley R.R. v. Thomas, 132 U.S. 174, 188 (1889)).

[179] 179 INS v. National Center for Immigrants' Rights, 502 U.S. 183, 189-90 (1991) (citing Mead Corp. v. Tilley, 490 U.S. 714, 723 (1989); and FTC v. Mandel Bros., Inc., 359 U.S. 385, 388-89 (1959)).

[180] United States v. Fisher, 6 U.S. (2 Cranch) 358, 386 (1805).

[181] Trainmen v. Baltimore & Ohio R.R., 331 U.S. 519, 528 (1947).

[182] See, e.g., Almendarez-Torres v. United States, 523 U.S. 224, 234 (1998) (words "criminal penalties" in section heading relied on as one indication that the section does not define a separate crime, but instead sets out penalties for recidivists); INS v. National Center for Immigrants' Rights, 502 U.S. 183, 189 (1991) ("text's generic reference to 'employment' should

be read as a reference to the 'unauthorized employment' identified in the paragraph's title).

[183] Trainmen v. Baltimore & Ohio R.R., 331 U.S. 519, 529 (1947); Intel Corp. v. Advanced Micro Devices, Inc., 542 U.S. 241, 256 (2004) (quoting Trainmen).

[184] Demore v. Kim, 538 U.S. 510, 535 (2003) (O'Connor, J., concurring) (citing INS v. St. Cyr, 533 U.S. 289, 308-09 (2001)).

[185] Yazoo and Mississippi Valley R.R. v. Thomas, 132 U.S. 174, 188 (1889).

[186] See, e.g., Donovan v. Dewey, 452 U.S. 594, 602 n.7 (1981) (citing the preamble to the Mine Safety and Health Act as evidence of congressional awareness of the hazardous nature of the mining industry); Gray v. Powell, 314 U.S. 402, 418 (Justice Roberts, dissenting) (citing the preamble of the Bituminous Coal Act as evidence of congressional purpose).

[187] "[T]he preamble may be referred to in order to assist in ascertaining the intent and meaning of a statute fairly susceptible of different constructions." Price v. Forrest, 173 U.S. 410, 427 (1899).

[188] United States v. Turkette, 452 U.S. 576, 588-90 (1981) (relying on RICO statement of findings and purpose, 18 U.S.C. § 1961 nt.). See also Knebel v. Hein, 429 U.S. 288, 292 n.9 (1977) (rejecting, in view of Secretary of Agriculture's broad discretion to administer the Food Stamp Program, and in view of broad purpose of Act to "increase [households'] food purchasing power" (7 U.S.C. § 2011), a holding that the Secretary lacked authority to determine that receipt of commuting expenses to attend a training program should be counted as household "income" determining eligibility for food stamps).

[189] "[N]o legislation pursues its purposes at all costs. Deciding what competing values will or will not be sacrificed to the achievement of a particular objective is the very essence of legislative choice — and it frustrates rather than effectuates legislative intent simplistically to assume that whatever furthers the statute's primary objective must be the law." Rodriguez v. United States, 480 U.S. 522, 525-26 (1987) (per curiam).

[190] Compare Justice Brennan's opinion of the Court in Mississippi Band of Choctaw Indians v. Holyfield, 490 U.S. 30, 50-51 (1989) (Congress used undefined term "domicile" so as to protect tribal jurisdiction in child custody cases), with Justice Stevens' dissent, id. at 54 (Congress intended to protect the parents as well as the tribe).

[191] Monahan v. Dorchester Counseling Ctr., Inc., 961 F.2d 987, 994-95 (1st. Cir. 1992) ("sense of Congress" that each state "should" review and revise its laws to ensure services for mental health patients); Yang v. California

Dep't of Social Services, 183 F.3d 953, 958- 61 (9th Cir. 1999) ("sense of Congress" that Hmong and other Lao refugees who fought in Vietnam war "should" be considered veterans for purposes of receiving certain welfare benefits).

[192] See Accardi v. Pennsylvania R.R., 383 U.S. 225, 229 (1966) ("sense of Congress" that reemployed veterans should not lose seniority as a result of military service evidenced "continuing purpose" already established by existing law); State Highway Comm'n v. Volpe, 479 F.2d 1099, 1116 (8th Cir. 1973) ("sense of Congress" language "can be useful in resolving ambiguities in statutory construction," and in reinforcing the meaning of earlier law).

[193] PMC, Inc. v. Sherwin-Williams Co., 151 F.3d 610, 618 (7th Cir. 1998).

[194] The "sole function" of a saving clause in CERCLA, the Superfund law, is to clarify that the provision authorizing a limited right of contribution "does nothing to 'diminish' any cause(s) of action for contribution that may exist independently . . . ." Cooper Industries v. Aviall Servs., 543 U.S. 157, 165-68 (2004).

[195] Even if there is no conflict, courts may construe a savings clause narrowly. See, e.g., City of Rancho Palos Verdes v. Abrams, 544 U.S. 113, 125 (2005) (relief is not available under 42 U.S.C. § 1983 as an alternative to a new statutory cause of action to enforce a new statutory right; a savings clause providing that the amendments do not "impair" existing law has "no effect" on the availability of section 1983 actions because no such relief was available prior to creation of the new right).

[196] See, e.g., 30 U.S.C. § 189, which provides that nothing in the Mineral Leasing Act shall be construed to affect the rights of state and local governments to levy and collect taxes on improvements and "output of mines." The Supreme Court relied on this language in holding that states may impose severance taxes on coal extracted from federal lands. Commonwealth Edison Co. v. Montana, 453 U.S. 609, 63 1-33 (1981).

[197] See, e.g., Merrill, Lynch, Pierce, Fenner, & Smith v. Curran, 456 U.S. 353, 386-87 (1982) ("saving clause" stating that an amendment to the Commodity Exchange Act was not intended to "supersede or limit the jurisdiction" of state or federal courts, placed in the bill to alleviate fears that the new remedies would be deemed exclusive, was an indication of congressional intent not to eliminate an implied private right of action under the act).

[198] Adams Express Co. v. Croninger, 226 U.S. 491, 507 (1913). Accord, AT&T v. Central Office Tel., Inc., 524 U.S. 214, 227 (1998). In City of Milwaukee

v. Illinois, 451 U.S. 304, 328-29 (1981), the Court held that the Federal Water Pollution Control Act of 1972 created a comprehensive regulatory program that eliminated previously available federal common law remedies. Savings language in the citizen suit section providing that "nothing in this section shall restrict any right which any person . . . may have under . . . common law" was irrelevant, since it was the act's standards-setting and permitting provisions, not the citizen suit section, that ousted federal common law.

[199] See, e.g., Geier v. American Honda Motor Co., 529 U.S. 861 (2000) (state common law negligence action gainst auto manufacturer is preempted by a federal motor vehicle safety standard in spite of statute's savings clause roviding that "compliance with" a safety standard "does not exempt any person from any liability under ommon law"). But see Sprietsma v. Mercury Marine, 537 U.S. 51, 63 (2003) (finding no such conflict reemption, and concluding that the Federal Boat Safety Act's savings clause, providing that compliance with ederal standards "does not relieve a person from liability at common law," "buttresses" the conclusion that the ct's preemption language does not encompass common- law claims).

[200] In this sense, the statutory phrase is analogous to a parent telling a child "don't under any circumstances leave the house until I return." The parent doesn't really mean for the child to remain under any and all circumstances, but instead assumes that the child will try to get out if the house catches on fire or some other emergency occurs.

[201] Oregon Natural Resources Council v. Thomas, 92 F.3d 792 (9th Cir. 1996). The court harmonized the "notwithstanding" phrase with other provisions of the act that pointed to the limiting construction.

[202] Id. at 796. The Three-Sisters Bridge saga offers another example. After a court decision had ordered a halt to construction of the bridge pending compliance with various requirements in D.C. law for public hearings, etc., the project was abandoned. Congress then directed that construction proceed on the bridge project and related highway projects "notwithstanding any other provision of law, or any court decision or administrative action to the contrary." The same section, however, directed that "such construction . . . shall be carried out in accordance with all applicable provisions of title 23 of the United States Code." The federal appeals court held that, notwithstanding the "notwithstanding" language, compliance with federal highway law in title 23 (including requirements for an evidentiary hearing, and for a finding of no feasible and prudent alternative to use of parkland) was still mandated. D.C. Fed'n of Civic Ass'ns v. Volpe, 434 F.2d 436

(D.C. Cir. 1970). Then, following remand, the same court ruled that compliance with 16 U.S.C. § 470f, which requires consultation and consideration of effects of such federally funded projects on historic sites, was also still mandated. 459 F. 2d 1231, 1265 (1972).

[203] See, e.g., Schneider v. United States, 27 F.3d 1327, 1331 (8th Cir. 1994). The court there rejected an argument that language in the Military Claims Act ("[n]otwithstanding any other provision of law, the settlement of a claim under section 2733 . . . of this title is final and conclusive") does not preclude judicial review, but merely cuts off other administrative remedies. Noting different possible interpretations of "final," "final and conclusive," and the provision's actual language, the court concluded that "[t]o interpret the section as precluding only further administrative review would be to render meaningless the phrase <notwithstanding any other provision of law.'"

[204] To be sure, not every potential roadblock can be anticipated and averted by narrowly tailored language, and broad language may be necessary to ensure that statutory purposes are not frustrated. But, in spite of the interpretation in Schneider, supra n.203, the "notwithstanding" phrase is a blunt instrument. The Trans-Alaska Pipeline Authorization Act is a better model for such situations. That act directed that the Pipeline "be constructed promptly without further administrative or judicial delay or impediment," specified that construction was to proceed generally in accordance with plans set forth in the already- prepared Final Environmental Impact Statement, declared that no further action was to be required under the National Environmental Policy Act, specified which subsections of the law governing rights-of-way across federal land (a law that had been relied upon in earlier litigation to enjoin the project) were to apply, and severely limited judicial review. See 43 U.S.C. § 1652. For a less complete identification of laws to be disregarded, and some concomitant interpretational problems, see Norfolk & Western Ry. v. Train Dispatchers, 499 U.S. 117, 138-39 (1991) (two dissenting Justices disputed the Court's conclusion that the exemption of a carrier in a rail consolidation from "the antitrust laws and all other law, including State and municipal law," comprehended an exemption from the terms of a collective bargaining agreement).

[205] What is usually at issue in these cases is whether a federal statute creates a right in a private individual to sue another private entity. Persons alleging that federal statutory rights have been violated by state or local governmental action may be able to sue state officials under 42 U.S.C. § 1983.

[206] Marbury v. Madison, 5 U.S. (1 Cranch) 163 (1803) (citing Blackstone's Commentaries).

[207] Texas & Pacific Ry. v. Rigsby, 241 U.S. 39-40 (1916).

[208] See, e.g., Cort v. Ash, 422 U.S. 66 (1975) (creating a four-part test to determine whether a private right of action was implied, one part of which was congressional intent); and Touche Ross & Co. v. Redington, 442 U.S. 560, 575 (1979) (calling congressional intent the "central inquiry").

[209] There may be plausible answers for some older statutes. Congress may have enacted the law at a time when the old rule held sway favoring remedies for statutory rights, or Congress may have patterned the language after language in another law that had been interpreted as creating a private right of action. See, e.g., Cannon v. University of Chicago, 441 U.S. 677, 710-11 (1979) (Congress patterned Title IX of the Civil Rights Act after Title VI, and believed that Title VI was enforceable by private action).

[210] "Our focus on congressional intent does not mean that we require evidence that Members of Congress, in enacting the statute, actually had in mind the creation of a private right of action. The implied cause of action doctrine would be a virtual dead letter were it limited to correcting drafting error when Congress simply forgot to codify its evident intention . . . ." This "intention," the Court went on, "can be inferred from the language of the statute, the statutory structure, or some other source." Thompson v. Thompson, 484 U.S. 174, 179 (1988). Concurring in the same case, Justice Scalia found himself "at a loss to imagine what congressional intent to create a private right of action might mean, if it does not mean that Congress had in mind the creation of a private right of action." Id. at 188. Justice Scalia instead advocated "[a] flat rule that private rights of action will not be implied in statutes hereafter enacted," explaining that "[a] legislative act so significant, and so separable from the remainder of the statute, as the creation of a private right of action seems to me so implausibly left to implication that the risk should not be endured." Id. at 192.

[211] See, e.g., Alexander v. Sandoval, 532 U.S. 275, 285 (2001) (there is no private right of action to enforce disparate-impact regulations issued under the general regulation-issuing authority of section 602 of Title VI of the Civil Rights Act; even though a private right of action does exist to enforce the anti-discrimination prohibition of section 601, the disparate- impact regulations "do not simply apply § 601," but go beyond it). For analysis of the whole topic, including the changing approach by the Court, see Susan J.

Stabile, The Role of Congressional Intent in Determining the Existence of Implied Private Rights of Action, 71 NOTRE DAME L. REV. 861 (1996).

[212] 2B SUTHERLAND, STATUTES AND STATUTORY INTERPRETATION, § 51.07 (Norman J. Singer ed., 6th ed. 2000 revision).

[213] Id. A clear example of a general incorporation was afforded by § 20 of the Jones Act, providing that in an action for wrongful death of a seaman, "all statutes of the United States conferring or regulating the right of action for death in the case of railway employees shall be applicable." As the Court explained in Panama R.R. Co. v. Johnson, 264 U.S. 375, 391- 92 (1924), this "generic reference" was "readily understood" as a reference to the Federal Employer Liability Act and its amendments.

[214] Alaska Airlines, Inc. v. Brock, 480 U.S. 678, 684 (1987) (quoting Buckley v. Valeo, 424 U.S. 1, 108 (1976)).

[215] See, e.g., 2 U.S.C. § 1438 (§ 509 of the Congressional Accountability Act of 1995): "If any provision of this Act or the application of such provision to any person or circumstance is held to be invalid, the remainder of this Act and the application of the provisions of the remainder to any person or circumstance shall not be affected thereby." These provisions are also sometimes called "separability" clauses. See, e.g., 29 U.S.C. § 114.

[216] Alaska Airlines, 480 U.S. at 486. Absence of a severability clause does not raise a presumption against severability. New York v. United States, 505 U.S. 144, 186 (1992).

[217] "A severability clause requires textual provisions that can be severed." Reno v. ACLU, 521 U.S. 844, 882 (1997). See also Hill v. Wallace, 259 U.S. 44 (1922); and Carter v. Carter Coal Co., 298 U.S. 238, 3 12-16 (1936).

[218] See, e.g., 25 U.S.C. § 941m(a) (§ 15(a) of the Catawba Indian Tribe of South Carolina Land Claims Settlement Act of 1993): "If any provision of section 941b(a), 941c, or 941d of this title is rendered invalid by the final action of a court, then all of this subchapter is invalid."

[219] But see, e.g., Zobel v. Williams, 457 U.S. 55, 65 (1982) (observing in dictum that, due to inclusion of non-severability language in an Alaska law, "we need not speculate as to the intent of the Alaska Legislature").

[220] See Israel E. Friedman, Comment, Inseverability Clauses in Statutes, 64 U. CHI. L. REV. 903 (1997). Friedman contends that "inseverability clauses are fundamentally different from severability clauses and should be shown greater deference." Id. at 904. Inseverability clauses, he points out, "are anything but boilerplate," usually are included only after extensive debate, and are often designed to preserve a legislative compromise. Id. at 911-13.

[221] United States v. James Daniel Good Real Property, 510 U.S. 43, 63 (1993) (failure of customs agent to "report immediately" a customs seizure should not result in dismissal of a forfeiture action).

[222] Liesegang v. Secretary of Veterans Affairs, 312 F.3d 1328, 1377 (Fed. Cir. 2002).

[223] Barnhart v. Peabody Coal Co., 537 U.S. 149, 172 (2003).

[224] Barnhart v. Peabody Coal Co., 537 U.S. at 161.

[225] In Peabody Coal, the Court held that a deadline in the Coal Industry Retiree Health Benefit Act for assignment of retired beneficiaries to coal companies did not prevent assignment after the deadline. See also United States v. Montalvo-Murillo, 495 U.S. 711 (1990) (failure to comply with the Bail Reform Act's requirement of an "immediate" hearing does not mandate release pending trial); Brock v. Pierce County, 476 U.S. 253 (1986) (Secretary of Labor's failure to comply with the statutory deadline for beginning an investigation about misuse of federal funds does not divest the Secretary of authority to launch a tardy investigation).

[226] See, e.g., NRDC v. Train, 510 F.2d 692 (D.C. Cir. 1975) (setting general guidelines, based on equitable principles, for courts to follow in mandating agency compliance following missed deadlines); Sierra Club v. Thomas, 658 F. Supp. 165 (N.D. Cal. 1987) (using the length of time initially set by Congress as the measure of how much additional time to allow EPA after the agency missed a deadline for promulgating regulations).

[227] The classic extremes are represented by Caminetti v. United States, 242 U.S. 470 (1917), and Church of the Holy Trinity v. United States, 143 U.S. 457 (1892). In Caminetti, the Court applied the plain meaning rule to hold that the Mann Act, or "White Slave Traffic Act," which prohibits transportation of women across state lines for purposes of "prostitution, debauchery, or any other immoral purpose," clearly applies to noncommercial immorality, in spite of legislative history showing that the purpose was to prohibit the commercial "white slave trade." In Holy Trinity, the Court held that a church's contract with a foreigner to come to this country to serve as its minister was not covered by a statutory prohibition on inducements for importation of aliens "to perform labor or service of any kind." The Court brushed aside the fact that the statute made no exception for ministers, although it did so for professional actors, artists, lecturers, singers, and domestic servants, and declared the law's purpose to be to prevent importation of cheap manual labor. "A thing may be within the letter of the statute and yet not within the statute, because not within its

spirit, nor within the intention of its makers," the Court explained. 143 U.S. at 459.

[228] "In aid of the process of construction we are at liberty, if the meaning be uncertain, to have recourse to the legislative history of the measure and the statements by those in charge of it during its consideration by the Congress." United States v. Great Northern Ry., 287 U.S. 144 (1932). On the other hand, "we do not resort to legislative history to cloud a statutory text that is clear." Ratzlaf v. United States, 510 U.S. 135, 147-48 (1994).

[229] "When aid to the construction of the meaning of words, as used in the statute, is available, there certainly can be no <rule of law' which forbids its use, however clear the words may appear on <superficial examination.'" United States v. American Trucking Ass'ns, 310 U.S. 534, 543-44 (1940). Justice Frankfurter, dissenting in United States v. Monia, 317 U.S. 424 (1943), made much the same point: "[t]he notion that because the words of a statute are plain, its meaning is also plain, is merely pernicious oversimplification." Justice Scalia explains why he opposes ready resort to legislative history: "Judges interpret laws rather than reconstruct legislators' intentions. Where the language of those laws is clear, we are not free to replace it with an unenacted legislative intent." INS v. Cardoza-Fonseca, 480 U.S. 421, 452-53 (1987) (concurring).

[230] United Savings Ass'n v. Timbers of Inwood Forest Associates, 484 U.S. 365, 371 (1988) ("only one of the permissible meanings [of an ambiguous phrase] produces a substantive effect that is compatible with the rest of the law").

[231] Compare United States v. Locke, 471 U.S. 84, 92 (1985) (a requirement that a filing be made "prior to December 31" could not be stretched to permit a filing on December 31) with Davis v. United States, 495 U.S. 472, 479 (1990) (phrase "for the use of" — a phrase which "on its face . . . could support any number of different meanings," is narrowed by reference to legislative history). In Locke the Court explained that "the plain language of the statute simply cannot sustain the gloss appellees would put on it. . . . [W]ith respect to filing deadlines a literal reading of Congress' words is generally the only proper reading of those words. To attempt to decide whether some date other than the one set out in the statute is the date actually 'intended' by Congress is to set sail on an aimless journey." 471 U.S. at 93. Despite the evident clarity of this language, three Justices dissented.

[232] See, e.g., Sedima, S.P.R.L. v. Imrex Co., 473 U.S. 479 (1985) (disagreement over the scope of civil RICO).

[233] Thunder Basin Coal Co. v. Reich, 510 U.S. 200, 209 (1994) ("The legislative history of the Mine Act confirms this interpretation").

[234] See Darby v. Cisneros, 509 U.S. 137, 147 (1993) ("Recourse to the legislative history of § 10(c) is unnecessary in light of the plain meaning of the statutory text. Nevertheless, we consider that history briefly because both sides have spent much of their time arguing about its implications."); Toibb v. Radloff, 501 U.S. 157, 162 (1991) ("even were we to consider the sundry legislative comments urged [upon us] . . . , the scant legislative history does not suggest a 'clearly expressed legislative intent [to the] contrary'"); Arcadia v. Ohio Power Co., 498 U.S. 73, 84 n.2 (1990) (rejecting reliance on legislative history said to be "overborne" by the statutory text). The Court has declared that it will not allow a literal reading of the statute to produce a result "demonstrably at odds with the intentions of its drafters," but in the same breath has indicated that it is only "the exceptional case" in which that can occur. Griffin v. Oceanic Contractors, Inc., 458 U.S. 564, 571 (1982).

[235] See, e.g., United States v. Granderson, 511 U.S. 39, 47 n.5 (1994) (dismissing an interpretation said to lead to an absurd result); Dewsnup v. Timm, 502 U.S. 410, 427 (1992) (Justice Scalia, dissenting) ("[i]f possible, we should avoid construing the statute in a way that produces such absurd results"); Public Citizen v. Department of Justice, 491 U.S. 440, 454 (1989) ("[w]here the literal reading of a statutory term would compel 'an odd result,' . . . we must search for other evidence of congressional intent to lend the term its proper scope").

[236] See, e.g., Frederick Schauer, Statutory Construction and the Coordinating Function of Plain Meaning, 1990 SUP. CT. REV. 231; Arthur W. Murphy, Old Maxims Never Die: The "Plain-Meaning Rule" and Statutory Interpretation in the "Modern" Federal Courts, 75 COLUM L. REV. 1299 (1975); Clark Cunningham, Judith Levi, Georgia Green, and Jeffrey Kaplan, Plain Meaning and Hard Cases, 103 YALE L.J. 1561 (1994).

[237] Wirtz v. Bottle Blowers Ass'n, 389 U.S. 463, 468 (1968). For examples of reliance on legislative history for guidance on broad congressional purposes, see Shell Oil Co. v. Iowa Dep't of Revenue, 488 U.S. 19, 26 (1988) (purposes of OCSLA, as evidenced in legislative history, confirm a textual reading of the statute and refute the oil company's reading); Wilder v. Virginia Hosp. Ass'n, 496 U.S. 498, 515 (1990) (reference to Senate report for evidence of "the primary objective" of the Boren amendment to the Medicaid law).

[238] United States v. Universal C.I.T. Credit Corp., 344 U.S. 218, 222 (1952). "Statutory history" as well as bill history can also be important. See, e.g., United States v. Wells, 519 U.S. 482, 492-93 (1997) (consolidation of a number of separate provisions supports the "natural reading" of the current law); Booth v. Churner, 532 U.S. 731, 740 (2001) (elimination of "the very term" relied on by the Court in an earlier case suggests that Congress desired to preclude that result in future cases).

[239] See, e.g., United States v. Riverside Bayview Homes, 474 U.S. 121, 136-37 (1985) (attaching significance to the conference committee's choice of the Senate version, retaining the broad definition of "navigable waters" then in current law, over a House version that would have narrowed the definition).

[240] "This Court generally is reluctant to draw inferences from Congress' failure to act. Indeed, those members of Congress who did not support these bills may have been as convinced by testimony that the NGA already provided 'broad and complete . . . jurisdiction and control over the issuance of securities' as by arguments that the matter was best left to the States." Schneidewind v. ANR Pipeline Co., 485 U.S. 293, 306 (1988).

[241] Pacific Gas & Elec. Co. v. Energy Resources Conserv. & Dev. Comm'n, 461 U.S. 190, 220 (1983) (noting that language had been deleted to insure that there be no preemption); INS v. Cardoza-Fonseca, 480 U.S. 421, 441-42 (1987) (rejection of Senate language limiting the Attorney General's discretion in granting asylum in favor of House language authorizing grant of asylum to any refugee); Doe v. Chao, 540 U.S. 614, 622 (2004) ("drafting history show[s] that Congress cut the very language in the bill that would have authorized any presumed damages").

[242] See, e.g., Reves v. Ernst & Young, 507 U.S. 170, 179-83 (1993) (RICO section proscribing "conduct" of racketeering activity is limited to persons who participate in the operation or management of the enterprise); Gustafson v. Alloyd Co., 513 U.S. 561, 58 1-82 (1995) (legislative history supports reading of "prospectus" in Securities Act as being limited to initial public offerings); Babbitt v. Sweet Home Chapter, 515 U.S. 687, 704-06 (1995) (relying on committee explanations of word "take" in Endangered Species Act).

[243] The dissent in Babbitt v. Sweet Home found legislative history that suggested a narrower use of the word "take," reflecting a consistent distinction between habitat conservation measures and restrictions on "taking" of endangered species. 515 U.S. at 726-30 (Justice Scalia).

[244] "The language of a statute — particularly language expressly granting an agency broad authority — is not to be regarded as modified by examples set

forth in the legislative history." Pension Benefit Guaranty Corp. v. LTV
Corp., 496 U.S. 633, 649 (1990).

[245] Puerto Rico Dep't of Consumer Affairs v. Isla Petroleum Corp., 485 U.S.
495, 501 (1988). The Court explained further that, "without a text that can,
in light of those [legislative history] statements, plausibly be interpreted as
prescribing federal pre-emption it is impossible to find that a free market
was mandated by federal law." See also Secretary of the Interior v.
California, 464 U.S. 312, 323 n.9 (1984) (a committee report directive
purporting to require coordination with state planning is dismissed as purely
"precatory" when the accompanying bill plainly exempted federal activities
from such coordination); Shannon v. United States, 512 U.S. 573, 583
(1994) (Court will not give "authoritative weight to a single passage of
legislative history that is in no way anchored in the text of the statute"); and
Roeder v. Islamic Republic of Iran, 333 F.3d 228, 237-38 (D.C. Cir. 2003)
(explanatory statement accompanying conference report purported to
explain a previous enactment rather than the current one, and could not
operate to abrogate an executive agreement). For what is arguably a
departure from the general principle, see Wisconsin Project on Nuclear
Arms Control v. United States Dep't of Commerce, 317 F.3d 275 (D.C. Cir.
2003) (relying on "congressional intent" relating to a lapsed statute). As
dissenting Judge Randolph characterized the majority's approach, "the
statute has expired but its legislative history is good law." Id. at 285.

[246] See "Statutory Silence," supra, p. 16.

[247] "[A] statute is not to be confined to the 'particular application[s] . . .
contemplated by the legislators.'" Diamond v. Chakrabarty, 447 U.S. 303,
315 (1980) (ruling that inventions not contemplated when Congress enacted
the patent law are still patentable if they fall within the law's general
language) (quoting Barr v. United States, 324 U.S. 83, 90 (1945)).

[248] Moskal v. United States, 498 U.S. 103, 111 (1990). Accord, Pittston Coal
Group v. Sebben, 488 U.S. 105, 115 (1988) ("it is not the law that a statute
can have no effects which are not mentioned in its legislative history");
PBGC v. LTV Corp., 496 U.S. 633, 649 (1990) ("the language of a statute
— particularly language expressly granting an agency broad authority — is
not to be regarded as modified by examples set forth in the legislative
history"). See also Oncale v. Sundowner Offshore Servs., 523 U.S. 75, 79
(1998) (male-onmale sexual harassment is covered by Title VII although it
"was assuredly not the principal evil Congress was concerned with"); and
Cook County v. United States ex rel. Chandler, 538 U.S. 119, 128-29
(2003) (local governments are subject to qui tam actions under the

expansive language of the False Claims Act even though the enacting Congress was primarily concerned with fraud by Civil War contractors).

[249] Edmonds v. Compagnie Generale Transatlantique, 443 U.S. 256, 266-27 (1979) (silence of legislative history "is most eloquent, for such reticence while contemplating an important and controversial change in existing law is unlikely"); United Savings Ass'n v. Timbers of Inwood Forest Assocs., 484 U.S. 365, 380 (1988) (major change "would not likely have been made without specific provision in the text of the statute," and it is "most improbable that it would have been made without even any mention in the legislative history"); Dewsnup v. Timm, 502 U.S. 410, 419 (1992) (Court reluctant to interpret the Bankruptcy Code as effecting "a major change in pre-Code practice that is not the subject of at least some discussion in the legislative history").

[250] Compare Justice Stevens' opinion for the Court in Chisom v. Roemer, 501 U.S. 380, 396 n.23 (1991) ("Congress' silence in this regard can be likened to the dog that did not bark") with Justice Scalia's dissenting rejoinder, id. at 406 ("apart from the questionable wisdom of assuming that dogs will bark when something important is happening, we have forcefully and explicitly rejected the Conan Doyle approach to statutory construction in the past").

[251] Sullivan v. Finkelstein, 496 U.S. 617, 631 (Justice Scalia, concurring in part).

[252] Mackey v. Lanier Collection Agency & Serv., 486 U.S. 825, 840 (1988) (quoting United States v. Price, 361 U.S. 304, 313 (1960)).

[253] REED DICKERSON, THE INTERPRETATION AND APPLICATION OF STATUTES 179 (1975).

[254] Red Lion Broadcasting Co. v. FCC, 395 U.S. 367, 380-8 1 (1969). By contrast, a "mere statement in a conference report . . . as to what the Committee believes an earlier statute meant is obviously less weighty" because Congress has not "proceeded formally through the legislative process." South Carolina v. Regan, 465 U.S. 367, 379 n.17 (1984).

[255] Mount Sinai Hosp. v. Weinberger, 517 F.2d 329, 343 (5th Cir. 1975), quoted with approval in Bell v. New Jersey, 461 U.S. 773, 785 n.12 (1983). See also Merrill Lynch, Pierce, Fenner & Smith v. Curran, 456 U.S. 343, 382-87 (1982), relying on congressional intent to preserve an implied private right of action as the reason for a "savings clause" on court jurisdiction. In FDA v. Brown & Williamson Tobacco Corp., 529 U.S. 120, 156 (2000), the Court ruled that, because legislation restricting the advertising and labeling of tobacco products had been premised on an

understanding that the FDA lacked jurisdiction over tobacco, Congress had "effectively ratified" that interpretation of FDA authority. The labeling statutes were "incompatible" with FDA jurisdiction in one "important respect" — although supervision of product labeling is a "substantial component" of the FDA's regulatory authority, the tobacco labeling laws "explicitly prohibit any federal agency from imposing any health-related labeling requirements on . . . tobacco products."

[256] Pierce v. Underwood, 487 U.S. 552, 567 (1988) (reenactment of "a statute that had in fact been given a consistent judicial interpretation . . . generally includes the settled judicial interpretation"). In Pierce, however, a committee report's approving reference to a minority viewpoint was dismissed as not representing a "settled judicial interpretation," since 12 of the 13 appellate circuits had ruled to the contrary. See also Metropolitan Stevedore Co. v. Rambo, 515 U.S. 291, 299 (1995) (reenactment carried with it no endorsement of appellate court decisions that were not uniform and some of which misread precedent); Jama v. Immigration and Customs Enforcement, 543 U.S. 335, 349 (2005) (neither of the two requirements for ratification by reenactment are present: the law was not reenacted without change, and the presumed judicial consensus was not "so broad that we must presume Congress knew of and endorsed it").

[257] Merrill Lynch, Pierce, Fenner & Smith v. Curran, 456 U.S. 343, 382 n.66 (1982), quoting Lorillard v. Pons, 434 U.S. 575, 580 (1978).

[258] Lorillard v. Pons, 434 U.S. 575, 581 (1978).

[259] Id. at 582. The Court "bluntly" rejects ratification arguments if Congress "has not comprehensively revised a statutory scheme but has made only isolated amendments." Alexander v. Sandoval, 532 U.S. 275, 292 (2001) (also expressing more general misgivings about the ratification doctrine's reliance on congressional inaction).

[260] Zenith Radio Corp. v. Hazeltine Research, Inc., 401 U.S. 321, 336 n.7 (1971). "[C]ongressional inaction is perhaps the weakest of all tools for ascertaining legislative intent, and courts are loath to presume congressional endorsement unless the issue plainly has been the subject of congressional attention. Extensive hearings, repeated efforts at legislative correction, and public controversy may be indicia of Congress's attention to the subject." Butterbaugh v. Department of Justice, 336 F.3d 1332, 1342 (Fed. Cir. 2003) (citations omitted).

[261] Although acquiescence and reenactment are similar in that each involves an inference that Congress has chosen to leave an interpretation unchanged, there is a fundamental difference: reenactment purports to involve

interpretation of duly enacted legislation, while acquiescence attributes significance to Congress' failure to act. Cf. INS v. Chadha, 462 U.S. 919 (1983) (Congress may legislate only in conformity with the bicameralism and presentment requirements of Art. I, § 7).

[262] In Bob Jones Univ. v. United States, 461 U.S. 574, 601 (1983), for example, the Court, in finding congressional acquiescence in a revenue ruling that denied tax-exempt status to educational institutions with racially discriminatory policies, pointed to inaction on a number of bills introduced to overturn the ruling as evidencing Congress' "prolonged and acute awareness of so important an issue." See also United States v. Rutherford, 442 U.S. 544 (1979) (finding acquiescence, and pointing to congressional hearings as evidencing congressional awareness of FDA policy). On the other hand, failure to include in an amendment language addressing an interpretation described as then-prevailing in a memo placed in the Congressional Record is "too slender a reed" on which to base an inference of congressional acquiescence. McLaughlin v. Richland Shoe Co., 486 U.S. 128, 132 n.8 (1988).

[263] "The 'complicated check on legislation' . . . erected by our Constitution creates an inertia that makes it impossible to assert with any degree of assurance that congressional failure to act represents (1) approval of the status quo, as opposed to (2) inability to agree upon how to alter the status quo, (3) unawareness of the status quo, (4) indifference to the status quo, or even (5) political cowardice." Johnson v. Transportation Agency, 480 U.S. 616, 672 (1987) (Justice Scalia, dissenting).

[264] Consumer Product Safety Comm'n v. GTE Sylvania, 447 U.S. 102, 118 n.13 (1980) (dismissing as not "entitled to much weight here" a statement at hearings made by the bill's sponsor four years after enactment, and language in a conference report on amendments, also four years after enactment).

[265] Southeastern Community College v. Davis, 442 U.S. 397, 411 n.1 1 (1979) (dismissing 1974 committee report language and 1978 floor statements purporting to explain 1973 enactment). See also Los Angeles Dep't of Water & Power v. Manhart, 435 U.S. 702, 714 (1978) (one member's "isolated comment on the Senate floor" a year after enactment "cannot change the effect of the plain language of the statute itself").

[266] NLRB v. Health Care & Retirement Corp., 511 U.S. 571, 582 (1994) ("isolated statement" in 1974 committee report accompanying amendments to other sections of act is not "authoritative interpretation" of language enacted in 1947).

[267] Bread Political Action Comm. v. FEC, 455 U.S. 577, 582 n.3 (1982) (1977 litigation affidavit of a Senator and his aide as to intent in drafting a 1974 floor amendment cannot be given "probative weight" because such statements, made after enactment, represent only the "personal views" of the legislator). But see North Haven Bd. of Educ. v. Bell, 456 U.S. 512, 530-31 (1982), citing a bill summary placed in the Congressional Record by the bill's sponsor after passage, and explanatory remarks made two years later by the same sponsor; and Pacific Gas & Elec. Co. v. Energy Resources Conserv. & Dev. Comm'n, 461 U.S. 190, 220 n.23 (1983) (relying on a 1965 explanation by "an important figure in the drafting of the 1954 [Atomic Energy] Act").

[268] 2Other controversial uses of signing statements, e.g., to allege the unconstitutionality of provisions or to direct administrators how to implement statutory directives, are beyond the scope of this analysis. For analysis, see CRS Report RL33667, Presidential Signing Statements: Constitutional and Institutional Implications, by T.J. Halstead.

[269] See, e.g., William D. Popkin, Judicial Use of Presidential Legislative History: A Critique, 66 IND. L.J. 699 (1991); Brad Waites, Let Me Tell You What You Mean: An Analysis of Presidential Signing Statements, 21 GEORGIA L. REV. 755 (1987); Marc N. Garber and Kurt A. Wimmer, Presidential Signing Statements as Interpretations of Legislative Intent: An Executive Aggrandizement of Power, 24 HARV. J. ON LEGIS. 363 (1987); Frank B. Cross, The Constitutional Legitimacy and Significance of Presidential "Signing Statements," 40 ADMIN. L. REV. 209 (1988); Kristy L. Carroll, Comment, Whose Statute Is It Anyway?: Why and How Courts Should Use Presidential Signing Statements When Interpreting Federal Statutes, 46 CATH U. L. REV. 475 (1997); The Legal Significance of Presidential Signing Statements, 17 Op. Off. Legal Counsel 131 (1993).

[270] President Andrew Jackson used a signing statement in 1830, and in 1842 an ad hoc congressional committee strongly condemned President Tyler for having filed a statement of his reasons for signing a bill (See 4 Hinds' Precedents § 3492), but routine use of signing statements began during the Reagan Administration, when Attorney General Meese persuaded West Publishing Company to include the President's signing statements with legislative histories published in United States Code Congressional and Administrative News. The Attorney General explained this as facilitating availability of signing statements to courts "for future construction of what the statute actually means." Address by Attorney General Ewin Meese, III,

National Press Club (February 25, 1986). Presidents since Reagan have continued this practice.

[271] See, e.g., Berry v. Department of Justice, 733 F.2d 1343, 1349 (9th Cir. 1984) (citing signing statement as well as congressional committee reports as affirming one of the broad goals of the Freedom of Information Act); Clifton D. Mayhew, Inc. v. Wirtz, 413 F.2d 658, 66 1-62 (4th Cir. 1969) (cited as elaborating on floor manager's explanation of good-faith defense in Portal-to-Portal Act); United States v. Yacoubian, 24 F.3d 1, 8 (9th Cir. 1994) (cited along with conference report to establish rational purpose of statute); Taylor v. Heckler, 835 F.2d 1037, 1044 n. 17 (3d Cir. 1987) (refusing to consider a signing statement that was "largely inconsistent" with legislative history on which the court had previously relied); Caruth v. United States, 688 F. Supp. 1129, 1146 n.1 1(N.D. Tex. 1987) (relying extensively on legislative history but refusing to give "any weight" to signing statements).

[272] Department of the Air Force v. Rose, 425 U.S. 352, 366 (1976) (quoting Vaughn v. Rosen, 523 F.2d 1136, 1142 (D.C. Cir. 1975)).

[273] A related analogy can be drawn from post-enactment or "subsequent" legislative history in the form of "isolated statements," discussed above, usually dismissed by courts as entitled to little or no weight.

[274] Clinton v. City of New York, 524 U.S. 417 (1998) (invalidating the Line Item Veto Act as inconsistent with the Presentment Clause of Art. I, § 7, cl.2).

[275] Signing statements allegedly have been used for this purpose. "[T]he president had used the . . . signing statement . . . to effectively nullify a wide range of statutory provisions even as he signed the legislation that contained them into law." Phillip J. Cooper, George W. Bush, Edgar Allen Poe, and the Use and Abuse of Presidential Signing Statements, 35 PRESIDENTIAL STUDIES QUARTERLY 515 (2005).

[276] Garber and Wimmer, supra n.269, at 376.

[277] "It may . . . be appropriate for the President, when signing legislation, to explain what his (and Congress's) intention was in making the legislation law, particularly if the Administration has played a significant part in moving the legislation through Congress." 17 Op. Off. Legal Counsel supra, at 136.

[278] " [T]hough in some circumstances there is room for doubt as to the weight to be accorded a presidential signing statement in illuminating congressional intent . . . , President Reagan's views are significant here because the

Executive Branch participated in the negotiation of the compromise legislation." United States v. Story, 891 F.2d 988, 994 (2d Cir. 1989).

[279] Supra, p. 23.

[280] If Congress has directed that the President rather than an agency implement a statute, then, by analogy, it can be argued that Congress has implicitly delegated to the President whatever policymaking authority is necessary to fill in gaps and implement the statutory rule. But here again, the signing statement would not usually constitute an act of implementation.

[281] The Constitution's vesting in the President of the executive power and of the duty to "take care that the laws be faithfully executed" implies authority to interpret the law in order to determine how to execute it, but this implicit authority would not appear to require change to the Chevron/Skidmore deference approaches.

INDEX

sales, 8
sanctions, 27
satisfaction, 4
savings, 24, 25, 52, 63, 64, 73
search, 21, 70
Secretary of Agriculture, 62
Secretary of Transportation, 6
securities, 48
Securities Exchange Act, 58, 60
security, 60
seizure, 68
self-government, 61
semantic, 29
Senate, 36, 70, 71, 75
sentences, 60
services, 43, 62
sex, 50
sexual harassment, 72
Shell, 48, 70
Sherman Act, 51, 54, 59
sign, 35
silver, 43
singular, 6, 45
sites, 65
slave trade, 68
Social Security, 41, 48, 55, 60
Social Services, 63
South Carolina, 67, 73
South Dakota, 43, 55, 56
sovereignty, 14, 61
species, 71
spelling, 25
sponsor, 75, 76
sporadic, 51
standards, 39, 50, 64
state control, 53
state laws, 43, 48
state planning, 72
statutes, x, 4, 5, 6, 7, 8, 9, 10, 15, 16, 19, 20,
    21, 22, 32, 35, 36, 39, 40, 41, 44, 45, 47,
    50, 57, 58, 61, 66, 67, 74
statutory, ix, x, 1, 2, 3, 4, 5, 6, 7, 8, 9, 10, 13,
    15, 17, 18, 20, 24, 25, 27, 29, 30, 32, 35,
    36, 39, 40, 41, 42, 43, 46, 47, 48, 50, 51,

52, 54, 55, 56, 61, 63, 64, 65, 66, 68, 69,
    70, 73, 74, 76, 77, 78
statutory provisions, 77
stock, 40
substitution, 45
Superfund, 63
supervision, 74
Supreme Court, ix, x, 1, 2, 4, 5, 17, 18, 21, 26,
    29, 35, 40, 52, 63
sympathetic, 5
syntax, 21, 46

T

tanks, 40
tariff, 43
taxation, 8, 53
taxes, 63
tax-exempt, 75
telecommunications, 43, 48
Tennessee, 54
Tennessee Valley Authority, 54
tension, 57
territorial, 16, 53
testimony, 71
Texas, 66
timber, 25
time, x, 4, 6, 8, 18, 20, 26, 33, 35, 40, 41, 66,
    68, 70
timing, 27
title, 23, 26, 62, 64, 65, 67
tobacco, 10, 18, 51, 56, 73
tort, 51
trade, 68
trading, 5
tradition, 4, 59
training, 62
transportation, 68
trend, 29
trial, 10, 53, 68
tribal, 22, 61, 62
tribes, 22
TVA, 58